AF469403

Death in London

First published 2007

by Historical Publications Ltd
32 Ellington Street, London N7 8PL
(Tel: 020 7607 1628)

ISBN 978-1-905286-22-5
British Library Cataloguing-in-Publication Data
A catalogue record for this book is available from the British Library

Typeset in Book Antiqua by Historical Publications Ltd
Reproduction by Tintern Graphics
Printed by Edelvives, Zaragoza, Spain

The Illustrations

The following kindly gave permission to reproduce illustrations:
Robert Bard: *1, 5, 7, 8, 11, 13, 20, 21, 24, 26, 28, 29, 39, 42, 43, 47, 50, 51, 53, 54, 56, 57, 58, 59, 63, 66, 67, 69, 71, 90, 93, 94, 95, 95a, 98, 99, 100, 104, 110, 111, 112, 115, 118, 120, 123, 124*
Guildhall Library, Prints and Drawings, London: *2*
© National Portrait Gallery, London: *55*

Other illustrations were supplied by the Publisher.

The illustration on the front jacket is of the execution of the Jacobite Lords Balmerino and Kilmarnock at Tower Hill in 1746.
It is reproduced by kind permission of the Museum of London.

DEATH
in London

Places of Execution, then and now

Robert Bard

Contents

INTRODUCTION

London and its Executions

Executions always held a fascination for Londoners. There were numerous execution places, the best known such as Tower Hill and Tyburn, but there were others used less frequently such as Smithfield, Charing Cross, Kennington Common, Shepherds Bush, and St Paul's churchyard. Some were used only once such as those where the felon was executed at the scene of his crime. It was this custom which brought Patrick McCarty to execution at the bottom of Bow Street, Covent Garden, Westminster, on 24 October, 1760, for murder.

A nineteenth-century history of London commented that the London of the eighteenth century had been called 'the City of the Gallows.'[1] The author, writing at a time when public executions were part of a festive landscape, remarked that you could

> 'enter it [London] at any point, and you would have to pass under a line of gibbets. Pass up the Thames, there were the gibbets along its banks ... Land at Execution Dock [Wapping], and a gallows was being erected for the punishment of some offender ... Enter from the west by Oxford-street, and there was the gallows-tree at Tyburn ... Cross any of the heaths, commons, or forests near London, and you would be startled by the creaking of the chains from which some gibbeted highwayman was dropping piecemeal ... Nay, the gallows was set up before your own door in every part of the town ...'

The public nature of executions and the entertainment they provided was recorded by a Swiss tourist, Thomas Platter (d. 1582), whose English travel record was published in 1599:

> 'This city of London is not only brimful of curiosities but so populous also that one simply cannot walk along the streets for the crowd. Especially every quarter when the law courts sit in London and they throng from all parts of England for the terms to litigate in numerous matters which have occurred in the interim, for everything is saved up till that time; then there is a slaughtering and a hanging, and from all the prisons (of which there are several scattered about the town where they ask alms of the passers by, and sometimes they collect so much by their begging that they can purchase their freedom) people are taken and tried; when the trial is over, those condemned to the rope are placed on a cart, each one with a rope about his neck, and the hangman drives with them out of the town to the gallows, called Tyburn, almost an hour away from the city; there he fastens them up one after another by the rope and drives the cart off under the gallows, which is not very high off the ground; then the criminals' friends come and draw them down by their feet, that they may die all the sooner. They are then taken down from the gallows and buried in the neighbouring cemetery, where a house stands haunted by such monsters that no one can live in it, and I myself saw it. Rarely does a law day in London in all the four sessions pass without some twenty to thirty persons – both men and women – being gibbeted.'

Death and the instruments of death and punishment were confronted at every turn. The execution sites, often at major crossroads, were intended to remind the lawless classes and anyone in danger of offending authority that the state held the ultimate power of life and death.

1. *The frontispiece to* The Malefactor's Register or the Newgate Calendar. *A mother points out a gibbet to her child – a consequence of a criminal life.*

The state ostensibly executed either to rid itself of opponents it saw as a political threat, or to preserve the rights of property owners. Public executions were meant to be a warning to those considering a life of crime. The reality, as described by a number of 18th- and 19th-century observers was quite different. Public executions were little more than public carnivals in which traditions evolved that allowed the condemned his or her last fifteen minutes of fame, and the public their entertainment. This was portrayed vividly in Hogarth's *Industry and Idleness* series. The same 19th-century author remarks that Hogarth's images of the Tyburn procession must have been in reality a 'strange sight', frequent enough to elicit indifference from many spectators.[2] Charles Dickens, a vehement campaigner against public execution, believed the entire process and ritual to be pointless and demeaning. He posed, rhetorically, the question whether those who attended executions were put off crime:

> 'There never is (and there never was) an execution at the Old Bailey in London, but the spectators include two large classes of thieves – one class who go there as they would go to a dog-fight, or any other brutal sport, for the attraction and excitement of the spectacle; the other who make it a dry matter of business, and mix with the crowd solely to pick pockets. Add to these, the dissolute, the drunken, the most idle, profligate, and abandoned of both sexes – some moody ill-conditioned minds, drawn thither by a fearful interest – and some impelled by curiosity; of whom the greater part are of an age and temperament rendering the gratification of that curiosity highly dangerous to themselves and to society ....'[3]

The London mob turned out in large numbers to witness executions, in rare cases up to 100,000 attending a single event, but more typically between 3000 and 40,000. Generally, it was the young, the poor and the members of London's large underclass who provided the actors for this ultimate form of entertainment. The majority of the more affluent and those of a better social class escaped with fines, or at worst, a more dignified form of execution. The hanging of Earl Ferrers at Tyburn in 1760 for the murder of his steward was a notable exception to this, though even here Ferrers was allowed to have a more prestigious exit, arriving at Tyburn in his own horse and carriage, still waited on by his servants. The only compensation for the lower orders, despite the horrors of death, was a chance to exit bravely in front of a large and sympathetic crowd, so as to leave some mark on memory or posterity.

Rituals and expectations associated with executions developed over the centuries. It was important that the victim should undergo a 'good death', which meant showing bravado and an indifference to one's fate and to offer the public an entertaining final speech. These were often transcribed and sold to the waiting mob – frequently before they were actually spoken. A generic form of 'death literature' evolved. However, the reality is that the majority of felons were so scared that many couldn't even speak or stand during their last minutes. Some even had to be seated to be hanged. Some of them were popular with the crowd and excited pity and shouts of support, others aroused jeers and were pelted.

Descriptions of crimes and punishments were popular in 18th- and 19th-century middle-class homes. *The Newgate Calendar*, a series of volumes which detailed the lives and deaths of many criminals, often shared the bookshelves of the affluent together with the *Bible*, Foxe's *Book of Martyrs* and Bunyan's *Pilgrim's Progress* between 1750 and 1850. Children were encouraged to read it in the hope that it would inculcate sufficient dread of a life of crime. The editors of one version included as a frontispiece a picture of a devoted mother *(see illustration page 6)* giving a copy to her young son whilst pointing out of the window at a gibbet.

The *Calendar*, or *Malefactor's Bloody Register* was originally published in five volumes in 1760 dealing with crimes between 1700 and 1760. It appeared in many further editions, from

1820 as *The Newgate Calendar*. Between 1863 and 1865 it was published weekly as the '*New Newgate Calendar*.' Accounts of executions and the dying words of the condemned were printed and sold as popular literature in the form of broadsheets or chapbooks (cheapbooks). As will be seen when looking at the individual sites of execution and their associated rituals, the condemned were subjected to a tortuous and drawn out final journey, the best documented of which was that from Newgate Gaol to the gallows three miles away at Tyburn. It was customary for the procession of carts, usually two or three with the prisoners and their coffins, along with a chaplain to stop en-route from Newgate to Tyburn at St Sepulchre Church opposite Newgate, where friends would present the condemned with bouquets which would be stuck on their breast button holes, acting as a nose-gay. This tradition continued until 1774. The procession, followed by a heaving crowd, would then move on and stop in Holborn, and then at St. Giles-in-the-Fields near the site of today's Centre Point. Here the condemned had a final cup of ale. There are many contemporary comments that suggest that the felons were launched into eternity 'in a state of wild intoxication.'[4] Inevitably, a mixture of alcohol and bravado led to frequent interchanges between the crowd and the condemned. The *London Magazine* of July 1735 tells us that at an execution on the 21st of that month,[5] 'five of the condemned malefactors were executed at Tyburn ...' there being two carts and a coach, the occupants of the second cart 'behaved very audaciously, calling out to the populace, and laughing aloud several times ...' though the magazine optimistically commented that alcohol could not have played a part as it was banned by the Lord Mayor and Aldermen.

The crowds gathering to see these executions comprised people of all classes. The upper echelons of society paid large sums for exclusive viewing points near to and around the gallows at Tyburn, Newgate, and Tower Hill, while the mob jostled to get as close as possible. At the execution of Charles I in 1649, despite the construction of a scaffold designed to obscure the view of onlookers, the crowd, not to be outwitted, lined the surrounding roofs. Attending executions was a recreational pastime: some of London's most prominent citizens have left accounts of attending them. Samuel Pepys, observed the hanging of a Colonel James Turner, whom he happened to know, and failed to see the irony when he, Pepys, seemed more concerned with his own discomfort in the crowd than that of his former acquaintance about to be hanged. He wrote in his diary:

> '21 January 1664. Up; and after sending my wife to my aunt Wight's to get a place to see Turner hanged, I to the office, where we sat all the morning. And at noon, going to the Change and seeing people flock in that, I enquired and found that Turner was not yet hanged; and so I went among them to Leadenhall Street at the end of Lyme Street, near where the robbery was done, and so to St Mary Axe, where he lived; and there I got for a shilling to stand upon the wheel of a cart, in great pain, above an hour before the execution was done....'

It was not until the middle of the nineteenth century that there was a noticeable shift amongst the educated classes that led to a questioning of the morality that allowed a Christian country to enjoy the suffering of fellow human beings. Dickens wrote a letter to the *Times* of 13 November 1849 expressing his horror at attending the execution of a husband and wife, Mr. and Mrs. Manning, at Horsemonger Lane Gaol.

> 'I was a witness of the execution at Horsemonger Lane this morning. I went there with the intention of observing the crowd gathered to behold it, and I had excellent opportunities of doing so, at intervals all through the night, and continuously from day-break until after the spectacle was over ... I believe that a sight so inconceivably awful as the wickedness and levity of the immense crowd collected at that execution this morning could be imagined by no man, and could be presented in no heathen land under the sun. The horrors of the gibbet and of the crime which brought the

2. The execution of a parliamentary Colonel James Turner, convicted of having burgled the premises of Francis Tryon, a Lime Street merchant. The audience included Samuel Pepys.

3. Mrs Manning, whom Dickens saw executed in 1849.

wretched murderers to it faded in my mind before the atrocious bearing, looks, and language of the assembled spectators. When I came upon the scene at midnight, the shrillness of the cries and howls that were raised from time to time, denoting that they came from a concourse of boys and girls already assembled in the best places, made my blood run cold. As the night went on, screeching, and laughing, and yelling in strong chorus of parodies on negro melodies, with substitutions of 'Mrs. Manning' for 'Susannah', and the like, were added to these. When the day dawned, thieves, low prostitutes, ruffians, and vagabonds of every kind, flocked on to the ground, with every variety of offensive and foul behaviour. Fightings, faintings, whistlings, imitations of Punch, brutal jokes, tumultuous demonstrations of indecent delight when swooning women were dragged out of the crowd by the police, with their dresses disordered, gave a new zest to the general entertainment. When the sun rose brightly - as it did – it gilded thousands upon thousands of upturned faces, so inexpressibly odious in their brutal mirth or callousness, that a man had cause to feel ashamed of the shape he wore, and to shrink from himself, as fashioned in the image of the Devil. When the two miserable creatures who attracted all this ghastly sight about them were turned quivering into the air, there was no more emotion, no more pity, no more thought that two immortal souls had gone to judgement, no more restraint in any of the previous obscenities, than if the name of Christ had never been heard in this world, and there were no belief among men but that they perished like the beasts.'

Undoubtedly the brutalized mob reaction that Dickens despised was a result of the overwhelming presence of death in society – from disease, from childbirth, from poverty. A mother of twelve children, for example, may easily have lost eight of them before they reached the age of ten. A walk round any parish churchyard today will confirm this early loss of life. Death came sooner rather than later for most people. Death was often communal, 'the deathbed was likely to be a busy and noisy place, even if for once the dying got to occupy the bed alone; it was open not merely to the immediate family but to other solidarities of which the dying person was a member.'[6] This familiarity with death, the acceptance of early mortality, was a strong feature of the 16th, 17th and 18th centuries, and it is hardly surprising that many people went to the gallows without the sympathy of their fellow Londoners.

Until the first decades of the 19th century when reform was in the air, few questioned the morality or ethics of attending such spectacles – they were simply part of the public scene, no different to watching juggling at Covent Garden on a Sunday afternoon. The debate concerning the rights and wrongs of execution as a punishment did not arise until men such as Lord Palmerston, Charles Dickens and William Makepeace Thackeray called for its abolition in the 1840s.

When I started to research the victims and visit the sites of their hanging, I believed that many of the victims, in particular Charles I, the Lords Kilmarnock and Balmerino, Sir Henry Vane and Lord William Russell, were extremely brave: they were principled people who handled their own mortality immaculately. It was not until I became immersed in this that I realised what the writer Leslie Poles Hartley meant by his observation that 'the past is a foreign country; they do things differently there.' Early London was a country of the past that we can now barely comprehend. The rules were different; the people were different; and society that regarded itself as superior and cultured instead lacked the veneer we call civilisation, and this allowed untamed and savage instincts to impregnate it. Even children were hanged and it was only after 1800 that this became unusual and warranted comment. The last child to be hanged in England was the fourteen-year-old John Bell for killing another boy and robbing the corpse. He was executed at Rochester in Kent in 1831.

Most of the sites I have looked at are in central London, but I have included Hounslow, and Kennington because they are both atmospheric and easily accessible. Kennington and the former site of Horsemonger Lane Gaol are a short distance over Westminster Bridge. The journey to Hounslow on the A4 is in itself a route that was littered with gallows and gibbets.

In detailing but a few of those to die at each site I have used where possible original eyewitness accounts as the language gives a flavour of contemporary thinking. Where possible I have used reports that penetrate the veneer of scaffold bravery and allow a glimpse of the bleak reality for people who had no future beyond the next few moments. Where available I have used old illustrations alongside my own modern photographs of the sites described.

1 A. Andrews, *The Eighteenth Century; or, Illustrations of the manners and customs of our grandfathers* (1856), p. 269

2 *Ibid*. p. 273

3 Charles Dickens, Misc.Papers Paper III part II. (available on www.gutenberg.orgctext 1435)

4 Andrews, p. 274

5 The traditional execution day was a Monday

6 Andrews, p. 128.

CHAPTER ONE

Execution and London Society: some grim realities

Death at the hands of the state has been the subject of increasing study. Modern academics have developed theories as to why capital punishment evolved in the way it did, and why the state so publicly disposed of its enemies. The rituals associated with execution have also received attention. It is postulated that the condemned man's dying speech, which usually admitted the crime and blessed the monarch, was an admission of the legitimacy of the power of the state by which he had been condemned. The social backgrounds of the victims have also been examined, as well as those of the people attending executions as if in doing so a key will unlock and explain why early society was so inhumane.

The paraphernalia of execution evolved. It not only staged entertainment for London society of all classes, but gave a level of support for those about to die. It allowed victims to immerse themselves in a well worn ritual in which there was little that was unfamiliar. This provided a shield against the reality of impending death, and, often, their bodily obliteration at the hands of the much despised anatomical surgeons who fought for their corpses – it was popularly believed that the soul departed from a dissected corpse could not go to heaven.

Between the 1680s and the 1720s the number of offences punishable by death rose from about 80 to over 350, though the number of executions did not increase in direct proportion because the sentence was often mitigated by transportation to the colonies, and in some cases pardons. The death penalty was meant to act as a warning but it is clear from the voluminous literature about crime and society between the 16th and 19th centuries, that for many the possibility of dying on the gallows was no more than an occupational hazard.[1] For some it was a chance to play a central, pivotal role for a morning and through bravado and repartee with the assembled mob be remembered in the ballads and chap books by future generations. Indeed many who would have died in total obscurity still survive to us by virtue of the *Newgate Calendar*.

London Crime

Peter Linebaugh in *The London Hanged* (1991) examined the judicial records to see which part of society predominantly suffered at the end of the rope. Unsurprisingly it was the poorest, London's underclass. He believed that the ceremony of death at execution sites had a deeper meaning and function. The crowds treated law and authority with contempt, and that those who reached the gallows were part of a struggle between the poor and the rich:

> 'The crime was well known; the culprit was selected as an 'Example'; each of the condemned would be known to different sorts of Londoners according to his or her trade ... The hangings were permitted and ordered by men of a ruling class who had studied the applications of death throughout human history and had power to apply that knowledge. The hanging was one of the few occasions (coronations were another) that united the several parts of government (monarch, courts, Parliament, City and Church). Equally important to the meaning of these awful dramas was the renewal of the 'social contract'. Most of those hanged had offended against the laws of property, and at the heart of the 'social contract' was respect

> for private property. It could therefore be argued that, just as each hanging renewed the power of the sovereignty, so each hanging repeated the lesson: 'Respect Private Property.'[2]

Thus Linebaugh asserts that the spectators and participants at an execution were part of a social power game between the propertied and the weak and the poor, and certainly London's execution sites provide a lesson in early class distinction – generally, the respectable died at Tower Hill, and the poorer sort at Tyburn or Newgate.

Methods and rituals of execution

Man has always been inventive in the methods used to despatch his fellow beings. One of the cruellest was that of being 'hanged, drawn and quartered'. This was usually reserved for those convicted of treason and, probably for reasons of modesty, applied to men only. Women convicted of treason were usually burnt at the stake. Introduced by Edward I, there are records of it having been used in 1241 against a William Maurice, and again in 1283. One of the best known victims of this method was William Wallace on 22 August, 1305, made famous to the modern public by his somewhat inaccurate depiction and execution in the 1995 film *Braveheart*. Some other notable victims, who will be looked at in more detail, include Guy Fawkes. At the Restoration the regicides suffered the same grim fate, and even three who had died a number of years earlier, Oliver Cromwell, Henry Ireton and John Bradshaw, were exhumed and their remains posthumously punished at Tyburn. The method of execution was still in use, but considerably toned down, as late as 1820, when the members of what became known as the Cato Street Conspiracy were brought to trial. Arthur Thistlewood and his five accomplices planned to assassinate the Prime Minister, Lord Liverpool and his cabinet when they were at dinner in Grosvenor Square, but they were arrested at 6 Cato Street, just off the Edgware Road as they prepared to carry out their intention. They were sentenced as follows:

4. The Cato Street conspirators apprehended in their loft above a stable. 5. A plaque on the building erected by the GLC.

6. The execution of the Cato Street conspirators in 1820. After hanging, their heads were severed from their bodies.

7. The former stable today.

'That you, each of you, be taken hence to the gaol from whence you came, and from thence that you be drawn on a hurdle to a place of execution, and be there hanged by the neck until dead; and that afterwards your heads shall be severed from your bodies, and your bodies divided into four quarters, to be disposed of as his Majesty shall think fit. And may God of His infinite goodness have mercy upon your souls'.

In this case, however, the 'drawing and quartering' was omitted from the execution, as was the 'drawn on a hurdle' but the victims were hanged and after death, their heads were severed.

In earlier times it was not uncommon for noblemen, or persons of high birth to be sentenced to this form of death for high treason, a term which encompassed crimes that ranged from sleeping with the king's wife, to clipping the coinage. It was traditionally the prerogative of the monarch, usually observed, to commute the sentence to beheading or hanging. Another sign of the monarch's benevolence would be the giving of permission to the victim's relatives to take possession of the remains and give them a burial. The sentence itself remained in law for high treason until its abolition in 1870.

But even beheading, often used for people of high birth, was not always straightforward. The headsman was optimistically expected to grant eternity with a single blow of the axe, though sometimes the man bungled it and several blows were necessary. Often he was incompetent. Margaret Pole, Countess of Salisbury, was in 1541 at the age of approximately seventy executed within the walls of the Tower, and reputedly chased around the scaffold whilst the executioner hacked at her, taking eleven blows to despatch her. Another execution on Tower Hill was that of James, Duke of Monmouth in 1685. The rebellious illegitimate son of the late Charles II, pleaded with his uncle James II for his life, but as a contender for the throne was shown no mercy. The executioner lost his nerve and struck five times, then pleaded with the mob, offering a large sum of money to anyone who would finish the job, but was forced under threat to complete it to the jeering of the surrounding assembly.

The despatch of the high-born would usually be within the Tower of London or on Tower Green, where there was some privacy, but the lower orders could expect to die of suffocation at the end of a hangman's noose in the more public places such as the Tyburn or Newgate gallows. For them, even burial was not guaranteed as many were handed over to the surgeons for anatomy instruction. Burial, where allowed, was often under or in the vicinity of the gallows at Tyburn, or beneath paving stones in Newgate Gaol. Nineteenth-century building works in the vicinity of Oxford Street and Edgware Road unearthed large numbers of human remains.

It was customary for an aristocratic victim to pay his executioner a sum of money to carry out the execution cleanly. This was often paid on the scaffold, and another purse held by the condemned's servant, to be handed over only if the job was done in a satisfactory manner. It was common for the victim to ask to see and feel the axe to ensure that it was sharp enough for the impending task. Charles I interrupted his final speech on two occasions to tell those on the scaffold who wanted to touch the axe to leave it alone.

Final speeches of the condemned often expressed conviction that they would sit in God's presence for the sacrifice they were making. This is particularly so in the 16th and 17th centuries in which last minute offers of a reprieve for repentance were sometimes offered, but were always turned down. The martyrdom of early saints set a precedent. It has been argued that the 'mutilation of the flesh of the saints might have a redemptive quality...'[3] Many of the regicides, those collectively held responsible for the death of Charles I in 1649, suffered the torments of hanging, drawing and quartering with astounding composure and bravery. The state trial records tell us that they showed no fear and affirmed that they had no doubts as to the correctness of their cause. At a time when they were likely to be hanged for a few minutes, and then cut down whilst fully conscious so as to view their own slow and painful dismemberment, these people held a certainty that prevented panic and allowed them to show to those witnessing, and hoping to break them, that they could still undergo a 'good death.'

However, Gatrell in his book *The Hanging Tree* (1994) observed that 'most felons went to their deaths in quaking terror' and if the process of execution had not been surrounded by its protective paraphernalia of ceremony and pageantry, the spirit of the felon might well have broken. He cites a number of disturbing incidents which illustrate the frailty of some of the condemned when faced with their final moments:

> 'Most people would mount the scaffold 'trembling in a very extraordinary manner', their 'whole frame ...violently convulsed', their minds 'bordering on stupefaction', having to be supported by officials. Elizabeth Godfrey, hanged for murder in 1807, went to the scaffold in a 'state of frenzy'. Greenacre in 1837 refused the attentions of the ordinary of Newgate bravely enough, but at the scaffold he 'was totally unmanned; all his fortitude had left him, he was unable to speak ... and the officer was obliged to support him or he would have fallen.' One of the five pirates executed in 1865 had to be hanged seated from a chair, too faint to stand ... The parodic splendour of the Tyburn procession should not obliterate the truth that at the end of it the law killed people who were powerless to prevent that outcome and whose bodies were dissolved in terror.'[4]

A common theme of the 16th- and 17th-century gentleman on the scaffold taken there for political or adverse religious beliefs was redemptive in tone. The speeches show a certainty with which we in the 21st century may feel less comfortable. The execution of Archbishop Thomas Cranmer in 1556 is one of the most outstanding examples of certainty and bravery. Cranmer, a Protestant, and Archbishop of Canterbury under Henry VIII, was imprisoned by the Catholic Queen Mary I and burnt at the stake on 21 March 1556. He had denied his Protestantism, but just before his death, at Oxford, he recanted.

COLLECTION

OF

Proceedings and Trials

AGAINST

STATE PRISONERS;

As well where they have had the Benefit of a Legal Trial, as where they have been cut off by Arbitrary Sentences,

From the *Norman* Conqueſt to this preſent Time.

CONTAINING

Upwards of two Hundred Caſes and Trials not comprehended in any Collection yet Publiſhed.

To which is added,

So much of the Characters of the Perſons accuſed, and the Hiſtory of their Times, as will diſcover the Motives of the reſpective Proſecutions, and the Juſtice of the Adminiſtration in each Reign, as well as the various Interpretations and Alterations of the Crown-Law during this Period.

Being a Work which gives great Light into many Obſcure and Controverted Points in Engliſh Hiſtory.

Compiled by the EDITOR of the Four Firſt Volumes of STATE-TRIALS in Folio.

LONDON:

Printed for J. WILCOX, at VIRGIL'S-HEAD, oppoſite the *New Church* in the *Strand.* 1741.

8. Collection of State Trials, *published first in 1741, it eventually stretched to four volumes.*

One of the most famous beheadings of the 17th century, which generates many books, articles and debate, was the execution outside the Banqueting Hall, Whitehall, of Charles I on 30 January 1649 which is dealt with in more detail in Chapter 5. The King's conviction and certainty that he was there to defend God's laws, and all that was dear to him is reflected in his final speech:

'If I would have given way to an arbitrary way for to have all laws changed according to the power of the sword, I need not have come here. And therefore I tell you — and I pray God it be not laid to your charge — that I am the martyr of the people.

'In truth, sirs, I shall not hold you much longer, for I will only say this to you, that in truth I could have desired some little time longer because that I would have put this that I have said in a little more order and a little better digested than I have done. And therefore I hope you will excuse me. I have delivered my conscience. I pray God that you do take those courses that are best for the good of the kingdom and your own salvations.'

This poses a number of questions. Did Charles honestly believe that his impending execution was merely a transitory phase in his existence from mortal to immortal? In the seconds prior to placing his head on the block, the following exchange, took place. It is between the King and Dr.Juxton, Bishop of London and long-time compatriot of the King:

'Then the King turning to Dr.Juxon, said, "I have a good cause and a gracious God on my side."

Dr. Juxon: "There is but one stage more! This stage is turbulent and troublesome; it is a short one ! But you may consider it will carry you a very great way; It will carry you from earth to Heaven! and there you shall find a great deale of cordiall joy and comfort."

King: "I go from a corruptible to an incorruptible crown, where no disturbances can be."

Dr. Juxon: "You are exchanged from a temporall to an eternal crown; a good exchange."[5]

Beyond death

In the 19th century there was a fascination for the examination of the interred remains of famous forbears. Dean Stanley at Westminster Abbey, for example, presided over the opening of a number of royal tombs. Nowhere is this more apparent in the events that took place centuries after the execution of Charles I. In 1998 (the late) Robert Partridge, a Civil War historian, wrote a book called *'O Horrable Murder', The Trial, Execution and Burial of King Charles I,* which dealt with the more personal and detailed side of the death of that king. It relates the preparations for his execution, the treatment of the body, the subsequent burial at Windsor, and the subsequent reopening of the coffin in 1813 by Sir Henry Halford, personal physician to the Prince Regent, in the latter's presence. This guaranteed 'thereby the most respectful care and attention to the remains of the dead during the enquiry.' A very detailed, somewhat gruesome report including a drawing by Halford, now in the National Portrait Gallery, of the king's head *(see illustration 55)* in semi-decomposed, but recognisable state after it was removed from the coffin was published, which will be looked at in further detail in Chapter 5. There were rumours immediately after the execution in January 1649, that the King had been secretly buried in the vicinity of Whitehall, and that the coffin which went to Windsor was empty. Halford 'stole' the king's vertebrae that had received the executioner's blow and, it was rumoured, used it as a salt cellar holder. Queen Victoria on hearing this demanded that it be returned to the coffin, which was yet again re-opened.

Many of the more educated diarists of the 18th and 19th centuries who attended executions and left accounts expressed revulsion at what they had witnessed. Agitation to ban public executions grew until in 1868 they were abolished altogether. It was perhaps inevitable that the last one was incompetently performed. The victim in this last affair was the Fenian, Michael Barrett, who was hanged for planting a bomb at Clerkenwell in an attempt to rescue Fenian prisoners held in the prison there. The bomb killed twelve people. Death for Barrett was not instantaneous. A newspaper report noted that 'two or three times when the officials considered the work to be done, the powerful frame trembled, and the knees shook convulsively...'

One writer, dealing with Newgate in 1909, suggests that 'the brutal methods of English criminal law, from the earliest records up to the Victorian era, were the result of the intellectual starvation of the populace.' He writes:

'The people were taught that the methods of their rulers were all-wise, and ninety-nine in one hundred, being unable to think for themselves or intelligently to express their thoughts, accepted the laws as they were administered and worshipped at the shrine of authority. But with the spread of knowledge came a broader grasp of the problems of life, the desire for education, and the revelation that all things were not necessarily ordered for the best because years of custom had familiarised them ... Hence, much of the cruelty and injustice of the law have passed away. Our methods are now comparatively humane.'[6]

The Reality of Execution

The reality of judicial death varied according to the means of execution, the efficiency of the executioner and the time it took. Anne Boleyn, who was executed in 1536 by a swordsman who 'smote off her head at one stroke', was relatively fortunate when compared to some of the victims of Jack Ketch, the executioner responsible for beheading Lord William Russell in 1683 and the Duke of Monmouth in 1685. Ketch was notorious for taking several blows of the axe to remove the heads of both unfortunates. He even issued an apology by way of a pamphlet in which he blamed the victims, one not having 'dispose[d] himself as was most suitable' and claimed that he was interrupted while taking aim. There was even some popular doubt as to whether an efficient headsman brought about instantaneous death anyway, and the ritual of holding up the prisoner's head and displaying it to the crowd was to show the possibly still 'aware' victim the scene around him so that he could know that he had been executed. It was often observed that the decapitated head still showed movement of the eyes and lips and was still 'alive' for anything up to twenty seconds after decapitation.

English law knew no bounds to its cruelty. There are records of victims being boiled alive at Smithfield, and bungled burnings where the female victim, who should have been strangled prior to being burned, was left to die an excruciating death because the fire had been set too early and the executioner was driven back by the flames. The victims who were hanged, drawn and quartered, were often alive and aware well into the proceedings. In this the hangman ensured that the victim was cut down from the gallows before he fell into unconsciousness, so that he could appreciate every nuance of his own stomach being cut open and observe his intestines being thrown into a brazier. This form of execution remained on the statute books into the 19th century.

Hanging as a means of execution

Death by hanging was often not instantaneous, and carefully calculated drops designed to bring death quicker were a product of the 1880s – even then a victim's heart could continue to beat for several minutes. But before that hanging could be a slow process – typically up to 30 minutes, but one hour has been recorded. Sometimes instant death could be achieved by jumping off the scaffold ladder, where this was available, thereby cheating the crowd of their entertainment. At Tyburn, the victim would be mounted on a horse drawn cart that would pass under the gallows. This would stop, a rope put round the victim's neck (if it was not already placed round his or her neck at the start of the procession) and the cart trundle off leaving the victim dangling, and slowly suffocating. Gatrell observed that victims often took a keen interest in the mechanics of how they were to be despatched so as to avoid a lingering death. Ings, one of the Cato Street conspirators hanged at Newgate, told the hangman, 'now, old gentleman, finish me tidily: pull the rope tighter; it may slip.' He then struggled on the end of the rope for five minutes.

Robert Hartley, executed in 1828 at Maidstone, told the hangman, 'Do not be long about it – let me feel what drop you have given me.' He then leant forward to try the length of rope, and said, 'that will do – the knot is too much under my jaw.' The executioner moved it towards the chin, when he said, 'It is now too much under my chin.' When the rope was adjusted, he said, 'Put on the cap now.' When drawn over his face, he said, 'Let me draw it off my mouth.'[7] Despite these precautions he struggled for ten agonising minutes. Often the hangman would pull on the victims legs to hasten the end and at Tyburn friends or family of the victim would push forward to the gallows and hang onto his or her legs to bring about a speedier death.

Returning to life

Hanging was not always a reliable cause of death. It was not unusual for the families of the victims to wait by the gallows in order to fight off the waiting surgeon's assistants and after reclaiming the body, they rushed it off to a nearby house so as to apply resuscitation which usually included blood-letting. Many a felon not due to be anatomised would request that his family or friends undertook such a task. A report from the *Daily Gazetteer* of 7 September 1736:

> 'Bristol, Sept. 4. At 12 o'clock yesterday noon, Vernham and Harding were carried from Newgate to the place of Execution on St Michael's-Hill, attended by the Under-Sheriff and his Officers, and the Constables of the City (in a cart, with haltars [*sic*] about their necks) the Divine who attended them having finished his last office, the cart drew away; but to the surprize of every person, after being both cut down from the gallows, Vernham was perceived to have life in him when put in the coffin, and some Lightermen and others, who promised to save his body from the Surgeons, carried him away to a house near the Ferry on St Philip's Backs, and a Surgeon being sent for immediately, open'd a vein, which so recover'd his senses, that he had the use of speech, sate upright, rubbed his knees, shook hands with divers persons that he knew, and to all seeming appearance a perfect recovery was expected.'

Vernham died that evening, but Harding survived and recovered fully, following which he was pardoned. It seems likely then that a number of victims who were buried rapidly after execution may well have been alive. Just as awful are the accounts of those unfortunates sentenced to be anatomised after death. There are a number of reports spanning the centuries of the deceased waking up under the ministrations of a 'surgeon'. The following is from Stow's *Annals*, of 1587 and reports the case of a felon sentenced to be anatomised who woke up on the surgeon's table and lived a further three days:

> 'The 20 of Februarie, a strange thing happened to a man hanged for felonie at Saint Thomas Waterines, being begged by the Chirugeons of Ln, to have made of him an anatomie, after he was dead to all men's thinking, cut downe, throwne into a carre, and so brought from the place of execution through the Borough of Southwarke over the bridge, and through the Citie of London to the Chirugeons Hall nere unto Cripelgate: The chest being opened there, and the weather extreme cold hee was found to be alive, and lived till three and twentie of Februarie, and then died.'

An event with a happier ending is that of the execution in Oxford, on 14 December 1650, and subsequent recovery of Anne Greene. She had been sentenced to die at the Oxford Assizes for the crime of infanticide. She had arranged as was customary, for friends to hang onto her feet and strike her chest whilst being hanged in order to ensure a quick death. The hangman fearing that the rope might break asked the participants to cease their activities. After waiting for around 30 minutes, her body was taken down, and placed in a coffin which was taken to the home of Dr. William Petty, a lecturer in anatomy, for dissection. When the coffin was opened, with Petty and his students present, there was not a little surprise when the 'corpse' took a breath. The intended dissection became resuscitation. Treatment for the deceased's post-death recovery was the placing of the body in an upright position, pouring hot drinks into the mouth, tickling the neck, and the rubbing of the hands and feet, followed for good measure by blood-letting. She was able to talk within twelve hours and was fully recovered after two days. She gained a pardon, married, and lived for a further fifteen years.

There was a report in the *Newgate Calendar* of a far more alarming nature. A surgeon working on an executed German criminal carried on the dissection of a felon who had shown signs of life because he had been 'hanged for so cruel a murder, should we restore him to life, he would probably kill somebody else. I say, gentlemen, all these things considered, it is my opinion that we had better proceed.'

On 5 December 1705 a convicted house-breaker, John Smith, survived execution at Tyburn. The *Calendar* informs us that he was carried to Tyburn 'where he performed his devotions, and he was turned off in the usual manner; but when he was hung near fifteen minutes the people present cried out "A reprieve!" Hereupon the malefactor was cut down, and being conveyed to a house in the neighbourhood, he soon recovered, in consequence of bleeding, and other proper applications.' It was inevitable that those present would ask the question as to what it was like to be hanged. Smith responded saying that 'when he was turned off, he, for some time, was sensible of very great pain, occasioned by the weight of his body, and felt his spirits in a strange commotion, violently pressing upwards: that having forced their way to his head, he, as it were, saw a great blaze or glaring light, which seemed to go out at his eyes with a flash, and then he lost all sense of pain. That after he was cut down, and began to come to himself, the blood and spirits forcing themselves into their former channels, put him, by a sort of pricking or shooting, to such intolerable pain, that he could have wished those hanged who had cut him down.'[8]

Some early observations on punishment in London

The prolific Tudor chronicler, Raphael Holinshed (*c.*1525-*c.*1580), having devised his *Chronicles* of the early English kings and queens, was given the even larger project of compiling a history of the world from the Flood to the reign of Elizabeth I. It was a task that needed assistance and not all of the work was written by Holinshed. A part of it published in 1577[9] was written by

William Harrison (1534-1593). In a section 'Of Sundry Kinds of Punishment Appointed for Offenders' he asserts that hanging was a humane form of execution, at a time when it was in fact slow asphyxiation.

> 'In cases of felony, manslaughter, robbery, murder, rape, piracy, and such capital crimes as are not reputed for treason or hurt of the estate, our sentence pronounced upon the offender is, to hang till he be dead. For of other punishments used in other countries we have no knowledge or use; and yet so few grievous crimes committed with us as elsewhere in the world.'

He then claimed that torture, or 'torment' was 'greatly abhorred.' This is not supported by the facts. Torture was a familiar part of the questioning of prisoners, particularly those that refused to 'plead'; they were crushed by weights until they either pleaded, or died.

> 'To use torment also or question by pain and torture in these common cases with us is greatly abhorred, since we are found always to be such as despise death, and yet abhor to be tormented, choosing rather frankly to open our minds than to yield our bodies unto such servile haulings and tearings as are used in other countries. And this is one cause wherefore our condemned persons do go so cheerfully...'

Harrison perhaps rather optimistically claimed that the humane manner in which prisoners were despatched to their deaths led the condemned to go to them 'cheerfully'. He described the methods of the law's most extreme penalty, that of being hanged, drawn and quartered.

> 'The greatest and most grievous punishment used in England for such as offend against the State is drawing from the prison to the place of execution upon an hurdle or sled, where they are hanged till they be half dead, and then taken down, and quartered alive; after that, their members and bowels are cut from their bodies, and thrown into a fire, provided near hand and within their own sight, even for the same purpose. Sometimes, if the trespass be not the more heinous, they are suffered to hang till they be quite dead. And whensoever any of the nobility are convicted of high treason by their peers, that is to say, equals (for an inquest of yeomen passeth not upon them, but only of the lords of parliament), this manner of their death is converted into the loss of their heads only, notwithstanding that the sentence do run after the former order.'

There are a number of cases where we see members of the nobility pleading with the monarch for 'mercy' and having their sentences commuted by the lenient monarch to that of beheading.

> 'In trial of cases concerning treason, felony, or any other grievous crime not confessed, the party accused doth yield, if he be a noble man, to be tried by an inquest (as I have said) and his peers; if a gentleman, by gentlemen; and an inferior, by God and by the country, to wit, the yeomanry (for combat or battle is not greatly in use), and, being condemned of felony, manslaughter, etc., he is eftsoons hanged by the neck till he be dead, and then cut down and buried. But if he be convicted of wilful murder, done either upon pretended malice or in any notable robbery, he is either hanged alive in chains near the place where the fact was committed (or else upon compassion taken, first strangled with a rope), and so continueth till his bones consume to nothing. We have use neither of the wheel nor of the bar, as in other countries; but, when wilful manslaughter is perpetrated, beside hanging, the offender hath his right hand commonly stricken off before or near unto the place where the act was done, after which he is led forth to the place of execution, and there put to death according to the law.'
>
> Witches are hanged, or sometimes burned; but thieves are hanged (as I said before) generally on the gibbet or gallows ...
>
> Pirates and robbers by sea are condemned in the Court of the Admiralty, and hanged on the

shore at low-water mark, where they are left till three tides have overwashed them. Finally, such as having walls and banks near unto the sea, and do suffer the same to decay (after convenient admonition), whereby the water entereth and drowneth up the country, are by a certain ancient custom apprehended, condemned, and staked in the breach, where they remain for ever as parcel of the foundation of the new wall that is to be made upon them, as I have heard reported.

Of rogues, whom he complains due to lack of war are getting more numerous in the land, Harrison observes that Henry VIII had a beneficial effect in keeping the number of 'rogues' in check:

'For there is not one year commonly wherein three hundred or four hundred of them are not devoured and eaten up by the gallows in one place and other. It appeareth ... how Henry the Eighth, executing his laws very severely against such idle persons, I mean great thieves, petty thieves, and rogues, did hang up threescore and twelve thousand of them in his time. He seemed for a while greatly to have terrified the rest; but since his death the number of them is so increased.'

The Audience

Attendance at executions was a popular London pastime, but it could be dangerous. There are many reports of scaffolds and spectator seating collapsing, or other misfortunes leading to the death of observers. A report from *The Post Man* of June 1698 relates an incident which took place almost opposite Newgate outside St Sepulchre's church:

'Yesterday 6 of the condemned criminals were executed at Tyburn, viz. Audley who killed the apothecaries wife, Price for forging Exchequer Notes, and Brown for burglary, these 3 went in a cart. Doctor Morgan and his brother for coyning, and one Cook for coyning; these 3 went in a sledge. Just as the cart with the criminals reached the corner of St Pulchers Churchyard, a great part of the wall (on which leaned a great many spectators) fell down to the ground, by which I hear one man was killed outright, and a great many others wounded, (some say 40) some of which mortally, and it is said 4 are since dead of their wounds. This accident put a stop to the cart, so that it could not pass the usual way, but was obliged to return towards Newgate, and so go through Pye Corner, into Smithfield, and down Hosier-lane into Holbourn. The barbers apprentice for ravishing a girl is reprieved.

James Boswell (1740-1795), the Scottish diarist, lawyer and author, could not resist attending an execution although the experience troubled him greatly. At this time he was suffering from 'melancholy' and it seems a rather unusual form of spiritual uplift to visit Newgate with the intention of observing condemned prisoners, and then travel to Tyburn on the following day to watch them being hanged. On 3 May 1763 Boswell decided on impulse to visit Newgate Gaol to 'see prisoners of one kind or other...' In the cells awaiting execution at Tyburn the next day were Paul Lewis, convicted of robbery, and Hannah Diego, convicted for theft. He watched them walk past him into the Newgate Chapel: 'The woman was a big unconcerned being ...' and 'Paul ... was a genteel, spirited young fellow ... an acquaintance asked him how he was. He said, "Very well"; quite resigned. Poor fellow! I really took a great concern for him, and wished to relieve him. He walked firmly and with a good air, with his chains rattling upon him, to the chapel.' The entry from his *London Journal* for the next day, Wednesday, 4 May 1763 reads:

'My curiosity to see the melancholy spectacle of the executions was so strong that I could not resist it, although I was sensible that I would suffer much from it. In my younger years I had read in the *Lives of the Convicts* so much about Tyburn that I had a sort of horrid eagerness to be there. I also wished to see the last behaviour of Paul Lewis, the handsome fellow whom I had seen the day before. Accordingly I took Captain Temple with me, and he and I got upon a scaffold very near the fatal tree, so that we could clearly see the dismal scene.

There was a prodigious crowd of spectators. I was almost terribly shocked, and thrown into a very deep melancholy.'[10]

Thackeray, a campaigner for the abolition of the death penalty, attended a hanging which continued to haunt him: 'I can see Mr Ketch at this moment, with an easy air, taking the rope from his pocket; ... I feel ashamed and degraded at the brutal curiosity which took me to that brutal sight; and ... I pray Almighty God to cause this disgraceful sin to pass from among us, and to cleanse our land of blood.'[11]

Henri Misson, a Frenchman with an interest in English customs, left an account that makes us ask whether much of the intended victim's participation was bravado, or the result of a familiarity with the gallows that allowed it to be treated with some contempt:

'He that is to be hanged or otherwise executed first takes care to get himself shaved and handsomely dressed, wither in mourning, or in the dress of a bridegroom. This done, he sets his friends at work to get him leave to be buried, and to carry his coffin with him, which is easily obtained. When his suit of clothes, or night-gown, his gloves, hat, periwig, nosegay, coffin, flannel dress for his corpse, and all those things are brought and prepared, the main point is taken care of, his mind is at peace and then he thinks of his conscience.'[12]

One of the better known descriptions of a hanging comes from a letter written by Charles Dickens which was published in the *Daily News* of which he was the editor.[13] It relates to the hanging in July 1840 of a famous murderer, François Benjamin Courvoisier, who had been responsible for the killing of Lord William Russell on 5 May 1840.

'I was, purposely, in the spot, from midnight of the night before; and was a near witness of the whole process of the building of the scaffold, the gathering of the crowd, the gradual swelling of the concourse with the coming-on of day, the hanging of the man, the cutting of the body down, and the removal of it into the prison. From the moment of my arrival, when there were but a few score boys in the street, and all those young thieves, and all clustered together behind the barrier nearest to the drop-down to the time when I saw the body with its dangling head, being carried on a wooden bier into the gaol – I did not see one token in all the immense crowd; at the windows, in the streets, on the house-tops, anywhere; of any one emotion suitable to the occasion. No sorrow, no salutary terror, no abhorrence, no seriousness; nothing but ribaldry, debauchery, levity, drunkenness, and flaunting vice in fifty other shapes. I should have deemed it impossible that I could have ever felt any large assemblage of my fellow-creatures to be so odious. I hoped, for an instant, that there was some sense of Death and Eternity in the cry of "Hats off!" when the miserable wretch appeared; but I found, next moment, that they only raised it as they would at a Play-to see the stage the better, in the final scene.

'Of the effect upon a perfectly different class, I can speak with no less confidence. There were, with me, some gentlemen of education and distinction in imaginative pursuits, who had, as I had, a particular detestation of that murderer; not only for the cruel deed he had done, but for his slow and subtle treachery, and for his wicked defence. And yet, if any among us could have saved the man (we said so, afterwards, with one accord), he would have done it. It was so loathsome, pitiful, and vile a sight, that the law appeared to be as bad as he, or worse; being very much the stronger, and shedding around it a far more dismal contagion.'

Reforms

The number of those executed in England can only be estimated, but Gatrell believes that between 1530 and 1630 it was 75,000. Towards the end of the 17th century increasing numbers were transported to the colonies. Apart from a blip during the latter part of the 18th century the number consistently reduced, continuing to do so into the 19th century when in 1837 a large

9. Samuel Romilly (1757-1818) legal reformer. Oil by Sir Thomas Lawrence, c.1806.

number of the laws allowing the death penalty as a sentence were scrapped.

Sir Samuel Romilly (1757-1818), solicitor-general and law reformer, attempted to change the criminal law, believing it to be cruel and illogical. Because of the large number of offences punishable by death, whether the accused went to the gallows, a transport ship, or served a prison term was totally arbitrary. Although the majority of trivial offences were commuted, the prisoner would suffer the trauma of having the death sentence read against him or her. Romilly recognised the injustice of such a system, and in 1808 he managed to repeal an Elizabethan statute which made it a capital offence to steal from the person.

Further attempts to repeal ridiculous laws met with failure – there was still opposition from the House of Lords. However, in 1812 Romilly was successful in gaining the repeal of a statute making it an offence punishable by death for a soldier or a mariner to beg without a pass from a magistrate or his commanding officer. Romilly's major contribution to the English legal system was to demonstrate the inadequacies of laws designed primarily to protect property, with little sense of proportion.

There existed a contradiction within a society in which an intelligent, fun loving and cultured monarch, Charles II, could enjoy the spectacle of the disembowelling and slow tortuous death of the regicides at Charing Cross. Colonel Harrison, one of the regicides, was 'dragged on a hurdle past Whitehall (where Charles I was executed) to Charing Cross where the statue of Charles I on horseback stands today. In the presence of a great concourse of persons, including the king himself and many ladies of the Court, he was hanged, cut down whilst still sensible, his intestines drawn out and thrown on the furnace, and his quivering body quartered.' Years later the king would listen quietly to the account of an execution he could have prevented, that of Lord William Russell in 1683. He was also happy to countenance the exhumation of Oliver Cromwell, John Bradshaw, and Henry Ireton from their graves in Westminster Abbey, and have them hanged and dismembered at Tyburn.[14]

All evidence indicates that death by hanging was merely an occupational hazard for many criminals, and that often the crowds themselves at executions would be infested with pickpockets and other assorted criminals. Bernard Mandeville (1670-1733) a philosopher and satirist wrote a pamphlet in 1725 titled *An Enquiry into the Causes of the Frequent Executions at Tyburn* in which he questioned their efficacy: 'The Multitude of unhappy Wretches, that every Year are put to Death for Trifles in our great Metropolis, has long been afflicting to Men of Pity and Humanity; and continues to give great Uneasiness to every Person, who has a Value for his Kind...'[15] He devotes a chapter against those who believed that the justice system and capital punishment acted as a deterrent. His target is execution day at Tyburn:

> 'When the day of execution is come, among the ordinary sinners, and persons condemned for their crimes, who have but that morning to live,

> one would expect a deep sense of sorrow, with all the signs of a thorough contrition, and the utmost concern; that either silence, or a sober sadness, should prevail; and that all, who had any business there, should be grave and serious, and behave themselves, at least with common decency, and a deportment suitable to the occasion. But the very reverse is true ...'

He rails against the abuse, swearing, drinking oaths, imprecations and jests by the administrators at Newgate but says that the most shocking aspect of all 'to a thinking man' is the behaviour of the condemned who,

> '...for the greatest part you'll find, either drinking madly, or uttering the vilest Ribaldry, and jeering others, that are less impenitent; ... the Hangman, impatient to be gone, swears at their delays; and, as fast as he can, does his part, in preparing them for their journey.'

Gatrell in his study of the scaffold crowd records that 'a royal duke attended Courvoisier's sentencing in 1840, in a court crowded with ladies dressed up to the eyes and furnished with lorgnettes, fans, and bouquets ...' and that

> 'on execution morning people of rank were admitted to Newgate's Press Yard after breakfasting with the governor, there as practised surveyors of form contemplating the demeanour of the victims on their fatal journey to the Debtor's Door ... The Duke of Cumberland attended the executions of Hepburn and White in 1811, along with Lords Sefton and Yarmouth ... The high people were still going to executions in 1866, renting windows for £25 ...'[16]

In 1832, the Punishment of Death Act reduced the number of crimes that warranted hanging by two-thirds and eight years later William Ewart Gladstone MP, a future Prime Minister, attempted to have the death penalty abolished altogether. By 1861 the number of punishable offences had been reduced to four: murder, arson in royal dockyards, treason, and certain forms of piracy. Charles Dickens increasingly used his access to print to call for the abolition of public executions. It was not until the 19th century that many of the more esoteric forms of execution such as hanging, drawing and quartering were relegated to sentencing ritual, and then finally abolished.

1 Maureen Waller, *1700, Scenes from London Life (2001),* p.309

2 Peter Linebaugh, *The London Hanged* (1991), introduction, p.xxii

3 P. Jupp and C. Gittings, *Death in England: an illustrated history,* (Manchester University Press, 1999).

4 V.A.C. Gatrell, *The Hanging Tree: execution and the English people, 1770-1868* (1994), Ch. 1.

5 *The Intelligencer. A Perfect Diurnal of Some Passages in Parliament,* no.288 Monday 29th Jan – Monday 5th February 1648. Note the old-style calendar date. Charles I was executed in 1649

6 W.E. Hooper, *History of Newgate and the Old Bailey, etc. (1935)* p. 75

7 Gatrell, p. 47

8 *The Newgate Calendar,* Folio ed. 1951 pp. 24-26

9 Raphael Holinshed. *The firste volume of the chronicles of England, Scotlande, and Irelande, conteyning the description and chronicles of England, from the first inhabiting unto the Conquest. The description and chronicles of Scotland, from the first originall of the Scottes nation, till the yeare 1571. The description and chronicles of Yrelande, from the firste originall, until the yeare 1547. (The laste volume ... conteyning the Chronicles of Englande from William Conquerour untill this present tyme.)* Imprinted for John Harrison. Book III, Ch. 6 (1577); Book II, Ch. II (1587)

10 James Boswell, *Boswell's London Journal, 1762-3;* ed. Frederick A. Pottle, (Penguin, 1966), pp. 274-275

11 Waller, p. 321

12 See Anthony Babington, *The English Bastille* (MacDonald, 1971) and Philip Collins, *Dickens and Crime,* (St. Martin's Press, New York, 1962).

13 Letter to the *Daily News* 28 February 1846.

14 There is today a plaque in Westminster Abbey marking the site of Cromwell's former tomb.

[15] Bernard Mandeville, *An Enquiry into the causes of the frequent executions at Tyburn: and a proposal for some regulations concerning felons in prison ... To which is added, a discourse on transportation; and a method to render that punishment more effectual*, (J. Roberts: London, 1725), p. 55.

[16] Gatrell, p. 65.

CHAPTER TWO

Tyburn

Tyburn is Britain's best known place of execution. In its near thousand years of existence, it has been estimated that the number of unfortunates who met their death there probably numbered in excess of 50,000.[1] At the junction of today's Oxford Street, Edgware Road and Bayswater Road, as late as 1783, this area on a hanging Monday was densely packed with rowdy mobs, pickpockets and sellers of pies and pre-printed final speeches. The crowds were immense and balconies along the route from Newgate, and in the immediate vicinity of the western end of Oxford Street, would have been crowded with the 'better sorts' waiting for the entertainment to begin.

Early History

It is likely that Tyburn's origin as a place of execution was post-Norman Conquest. William I, who reigned from 1066 to 1087, actually abolished capital punishment, but substituted it with tortures and mutilations that left felons without eyes or limbs. Marks, in his work *Tyburn Tree*,[2] thought that 'the institution of the gallows there probably dates from the reign of Henry I (1100-35). An earlier name for them was 'The Elms', a tree of justice for the Normans, which emphasises the period of foundation. In Smithfield too, another execution place, there was a place called 'The Elms'

The first reference to Tyburn as a place of execution is in the year 1108 and a probable execution here is noted in 1177. The first confirmed execution appears in 1196 when William FitzOsbert or Osborn, described as being 'skilled in law' was the victim.[3] Accused of sedition by the mayor of London and the king's Regent while the king was abroad on crusade, William resisted arrest, and, together with his mistress, took sanctuary in the church of St Mary-le-Bow in Cheapside. He was smoked out of this, sentenced at the Tower, and with nine accomplices hanged at Tyburn. We are told that 'the simple people honoured him as a Martyre, insomuch that they steale away the gibbet whereon he was hanged, & pared away the earth, that was be-bled with his blood, and kept the same as holy reliques to heale sicke men.'[4]

Another early victim at Tyburn was Sir William de Marisco, or Marsh, implicated in an attempt to kill Henry III by cutting his throat at Woodstock in Oxfordshire. Marsh fled to his island retreat of Lundy in the Bristol Channel, from where he engaged in piracy. He was eventually captured due to the treachery of his fellow band of thugs, and he and sixteen others were handed over to the king. He claimed to be blameless in respect of the plot on the king's life, and his flight to Lundy was simply to appease the king by his absence. The plundering was accounted for as a simple need to survive. But, just prior to his execution

> 'he poured out his soul to God ... with contrition and tears he admitted his sins, not seeking to extenuate them, but even accusing himself. Therefore the friar preacher, a discreet man, who received his confession, gave him gentle consolation, and dismissed him in peace, exhorting him to suffer his punishment with patience, as a means of penance.'

Of the punishment itself:

10. William de Marisco (William Marsh) drawn to Tyburn gallows in 1242.

First ... he was drawn from Westminster to the Tower of London, and thence to that instrument of punishment, commonly called a gibbet: when he had there breathed out his wretched soul, he was hanged on one of the hooks, and when the body was stiff it was let down and disembowelled, and the bowels were at once burnt on the spot. Then the miserable body was divided into four parts, which were sent to four of the chief cities, so that this lamentable spectacle might inspire fear in all beholders.'[5]

Location of the Tyburn Gallows

The exact location of what was London's most renowned place of execution is a matter of some debate, complicated by its site varying over the centuries. However, it is reasonably certain that it did not stand where Marble Arch is located today.

Alfred Marks, who has studied the records relating to Tyburn in detail, tells us that

'the first information of the site of the gallows other than the vague indication of "Tyburn" is found in one of the old chronicles, which tells that, in 1330, Mortimer was executed at "The Elms, about a league outside the city." The distance thus vaguely stated would apply about equally to any one of the conjectured sites from Marylebone Lane to the head of the Serpentine, at which writers have severally placed the gallows.'[6]

Camden's *Britannica* of 1607 contained a map which placed the gallows, depicted as a triangular structure, at the north-eastern end of Hyde Park with the word 'Tyborne'. This is in itself evidence of the now permanent nature of the gallows. The 'triple tree', a more sophisticated approach to the mechanics of hanging, was installed to cope with an Elizabethan crime wave in 1571. Its design was an efficient innovation: up to 24 persons have been recorded as being dispatched on the same day. The first reference to it comes with the execution of a Dr.Story. We are informed:

'The first daye of June [1571] the saide Story was drawn upon an herdell from the Tower of London unto Tiborn, wher was prepared for him a newe payre of gallowes made in triangular maner.'[7]

Marks believed that a controversial incident concerning the French Catholic wife of Charles I acted as a method of pinpointing the location:

11. Detail from John Rocque's map of London, 1746. The gallows can be seen next to the word Tybourn, at the junction of today's Edgware Road and Oxford Street.

> '....on June 26th of this year,[1626] Henrietta Maria, [the wife of Charles I] after a day spent in devotion, went with her attendants through St. James's Park to Hyde Park. Whether by accident or design she went towards Tyburn. Charles hated the Queen's French suite [courtiers], secured to her by treaty ... The courtiers made the most of the visit to Tyburn; it was averred that the Queen's confessor had made her walk barefoot to the gallows, "thereby to honour the saint of the day in visiting that holy place, where so many martyrs had shed their blood in the Catholic cause."'[1]

Following the political controversy that followed a Marshall de Bassompiere defended the Queen and by his comments, possibly fixed the site of the gallows:

'"I know of a surety," he said, "that you do not believe that which you publish to others." He declared that the Queen had not been within fifty paces of the gallows. He repeated the description of the place as at "the entrance of a high road" The words "the entrance of a high road" fix definitely the spot indicated, approximately, by Norden's Map.'[8]

Marks believes that the road or highway referred to can be no other than the Edgware Road.[9]

John Rocque's map of London, 1746 places the gallows near the junction of the Bayswater Road and the Edgware Road. By 1759, locating their position becomes less certain, for then a portable gallows was introduced which was 'put up on the day of execution and afterwards taken down.'[10] Evidence for the removal of the triple tree comes from the *Whitehall Evening Post* of 4 October 1759 which says:

> 'Yesterday morning, about Half an Hour after Nine o'clock the four malefactors were carried in

12. The Tyburn turnpike in 1813, looking east, where Oxford Street and the Bayswater Road meet.

two carts from Newgate, and executed on the new Moving Gallows at Tyburn ... The Gallows, after the Bodies were cut down, was carried off in a cart.'

The location of the gallows is a debate eagerly picked up by *Old and New London*, published in 1878, 95 years after executions had ceased at Tyburn and had been transferred to Newgate. The last execution at Tyburn took place in 1783.

'The exact spot on which the fatal Tyburn Tree was erected has been often discussed by antiquaries. It would appear, however, to be identified with the site of the house in the south-east corner of Connaught Square, formerly numbered 49; for in the lease granted by the Bishop of London, to whom the property belongs, this fact is particularly mentioned.'

The writer then quotes from *The Antiquary* of October 1873, in which a contributor wrote:

'I was born within 100 yards of the exact spot on which the gallows stood, and my uncle took up the stones on which the uprights were placed. The following is his statement to me, and the circumstance of his telling it: In 1810, when Connaught Place was being built, he was employed on the works, and for many years lived at the corner of Bryanston Street and the Edgware Road, nearly opposite Connaught Mews. My father, a master carpenter, worked for several years in Connaught Place, and on one occasion he employed his brother, I think in the year 1834; at all events, we had just left No. 6, the residence of Sir Charles Coote. It was at this time I said to my uncle, "Now you are here, tell me where the gallows stood;" to which he replied, "Opposite here, where the staves are." I thereupon crossed over, and drove a brass-headed nail into the exact spot he indicated. On reaching home, I told my mother of the occurrence, and asked if it were correct. She said it was so, for she remembered the posts standing when she was a child. This might be about the year 1800; and, as she was born in

13. The turnpike site in 2007, looking east along Oxford Street.

Bryanston Street, I believe she stated what she knew to be a fact. I well remember Connaught Square being built, and I also recollect a low house standing at the corner of the Uxbridge Road, close to No. 1, Connaught Place [Arklow House], and that, on the removal of this house, quantities of human bones were found. I saw them carted away by Mr. Nicholls, contractor, of Adams' Mews. He removed Tyburn toll-house in 1829. From what I have been told by old inhabitants that were born in the neighbourhood, probably about 1750, I have every reason to believe that the space from the toll-house to Frederick Mews was used as a place of execution, and the bodies buried adjacent, for I have seen the remains disinterred when the square and adjoining streets were being built.'

The article continues:

'The gallows itself subsequently consisted of two uprights and a cross-beam, erected on the morning of execution across the Edgware Road, opposite the house at the corner of Upper Bryanston Street and the Edgware Road, wherein the gallows was deposited after being used; this house had curious iron balconies to the windows of the first and second floors, where the sheriffs sat to witness the executions. After the place of execution was changed to Newgate, in 1783, the gallows was bought by a carpenter, and made into stands for beer-butts in the cellars of the Carpenter's Arms public-house, hard by.'[11]

The Carpenter's Arms is still there, at 12 Seymour Place.

Thomas Smith in his work, *A Topographical and Historical Account of the Parish of St. Marylebone* (1833), notes that the movable gallows were usually erected near the corner of Edgware Road and Bryanston Street ... but the place was not always exactly the same. Evidence for this comes from the *Gentleman's Magazine* of 29 August 1783 which said that 'the gallows were fixed about 50 yards nearer the Park wall than usual.' As to the location of the Tyburn turnpike, Marks tells us:

'When the turnpike was in its turn removed, its position was recorded by a monument placed on the south side of the road, somewhat to the west of the Marble Arch. It is a slab of cast iron, with a gable top, bearing on both sides the words, "HERE STOOD TYBURN GATE 1829," that being the date of its abolition. This monument correctly indicated the position of the gate, which stretched across the road: it was not intended to show the position of the gallows, which, however, it did indicate approximately. It was necessarily removed in the improvements carried out near the Marble Arch in the spring of 1908.'[12]

This stone can still be seen, with some difficulty, behind a mortgage poster in the window of Lloyds Bank at 195 Edgware Road.

The Tyburn Ritual

As has already been noted the ritual of execution was important because it reaffirmed the power of the state and the sanctity of property. It has been suggested that 'the ideology of England's rulers, with its emphasis on the sanctity of property rights, found its visible and material embodiment above all in the ideology and practice of the law. Tyburn Tree ... stood at the heart of this ideology; and its ceremonies were at the heart of the popular culture also.'[13]

Sharpe in his work *Last Dying Speeches* notes that 'public executions were carried out in a context of ceremony and ritual, and the reactions which they aimed to excite among spectators were evidently more complicated than mere terror.' Central to the Tyburn ceremony was the victim's last speech. Sharpe observes that the purpose of this speech was 'to remind spectators that the death of the condemned constituted an awful warning ...' The reality was a ritual in such a preconceived form, that there was a brisk trade at the site of execution in the last dying speech of the victim, or victims even though still alive and awaiting imminent death. Farewell speeches were expected and they usually followed a predictable well-worn form. Henry Goodcole, a part-time ordinary at Newgate, commented in 1618: 'dying men's words are ever remarkable & their last deeds memorable for succeeding posterities, by them to be instructed, what vertues or vices they followed and imbraced

14. 'The Idle 'Prentice Executed at Tyburn'. From William Hogarth's Industry and Idleness, *plate 11, 1747. The artist recreates the licentious atmosphere of a Tyburn execution. The victim can be seen in the cart with his coffin and a chaplain.*

and by them to learne to imitate that which was good and to eschew evill". Another pamphleteer commented that the 'people always expect a confession at the time of any man's execution."[14]

Some contemporary observations on the procession

Contemporary reports help us to understand what Tyburn meant to people. The novelist Samuel Richardson (1689-1761), wrote in the form of a letter from a 'Country Gentleman in Town' to his 'Brother in the Country' in which he described the emotions, senses and rituals of a procession from Newgate to Tyburn and the execution itself. Richardson began:

> 'Dear Brother, — I have this day been satisfying a Curiosity I believe natural to most People, by seeing an Execution at Tyburn. The Sight has had an extra-ordinary Effect upon me, which is more owing to the unexpected Oddness of the scene, than the affecting Concern which is unavoidable in a thinking Person, at a Spectacle so awful, and so interesting, to all who consider themselves of the same Species with the unhappy Sufferer.'

Richardson then described what happened:

> 'That I might the better view the Prisoners, and escape the Pressure of the Mob, which is prodigious, nay, almost incredible, if we consider the Frequency of these Executions in London, which is once a Month; I mounted my Horse, and accompanied the melancholy Cavalcade from Newgate to the fatal Tree. The Criminals were Five in Number. I was much disappointed at the Unconcern and Carelessness that appeared in the Faces of Three of the unhappy Wretches: The countenances of the other Two were spread with that Horror and Despair which is not to be wonder'd at in Men whose Period of Life is so near, with the terrible Aggravation of its being hasten'd by their own voluntary Indiscretion and Misdeeds.'

Richardson's description encompassed the prisoners leaving Newgate:

> 'The Exhortation spoken by the Bell-man, from the Wall of St. Sepulchre's Church-yard, is well intended; but the Noise of the Officers, and the Mob, was so great, and the silly Curiosity of People climbing into the Cart to take leave of the Criminals, made such a confused Noise, that I could not hear the Words of exhortation when spoken ... All the way up to Holborn the Croud was so great, as at every twenty or thirty Yards to obstruct the Passage; and Wine, notwithstanding a late good Order against that Practice, was brought to the Malefactors, who drank greedily of it, which I thought did not suit well with their deplorable Circumstances: After this, the Three thoughtless young Men, who at first seemed not enough concerned, grew most shamefully daring and wanton; behaving themselves in a manner that would have been ridiculous in Men in any Circumstances whatever: They swore, laugh'd, and talk'd obscenely, and wish'd their wicked Companions good Luck, with as much Assurance as if their employment had been the most lawful.'

The procession made its way to Tyburn. Richardson reports the shock he felt at the behaviour and scene at the gallows. What he describes resembles a bawdy social gathering on London's streets.

> 'At the Place of Execution, the Scene grew still more shocking; and the Clergyman who attended was more the subject of Ridicule, than of their serious Attention. The Psalm was sung amidst the Curses and Quarelling of Hundreds of the most abandon'd and profligate of Mankind: Upon whom (so stupid are they to any Senses of Decency) all the Preparation of the unhappy Wretches seems to serve only for Subject of a barbarous Kind of Mirth, altogether inconsistent with Humanity. And as soon as the poor Creatures were half dead, I was much surprised, before such a number of Peace-Officers, to see the Populace fall to halling and pulling the Carcasses with so much Earnestness as to occasion several warm Rencounters, and broken Heads. These, I was told, were the Friends of the Persons executed, or such as, for the sake of Tumult chose to appear so,

and some Persons sent by private Surgeons to obtain Bodies for Dissection.'

Some Tyburn victims

On 23 August 1305, William Wallace was executed. Although it is commonly believed that he met his death at Smithfield (where there is a plaque to his memory), it is possible, even probable that the sentence was carried out at Tyburn. Marks writes that Wallace was

> '... drawn from Westminster to the Tower and thence to Tyburn ... "the man of Belial," as he is constantly called in the *Chronicles*. Wallace was hanged on a very high gallows, especially made for the occasion ... The place of execution of Wallace was undoubtedly Tyburn. The court sentence also ordered that Wallace's head should be exposed on London Bridge. This is the first recorded instance of a head being exposed here.'

The following year the Earl of Athol, accused of rebellion against the king, died here on 7 November, to the delight of the ailing King Edward I and, as Athol claimed to be of royal descent, he was therefore, as a gesture from Edward, 'hanged higher than other parricides'. Royal blood had privileges, one being that he was allowed to ride on horseback to Tyburn, another that he was hanged on 50 foot high gallows. After being suspended, according to the chronicler, Matthew of Westminster,[15] he was let down, half alive, 'so that his torment might be greater, very cruelly beheaded, then the body was thrown into a fire previously kindled in the sight of the sufferer, and reduced to ashes. Then the head was placed on London Bridge among those of other traitors, but higher than the rest, in regard to his royal descent.'

Mistakes did happen. In 1386 three servants were 'mistakenly' hanged and drawn:

> 'The good man of the Cocke in Cheap at the little conduit was murdered in the night time by a theife that came in at a gutter window, as it was knowne long after by the same theife, when he was at the gallowes to be hanged for felonie, but his wife was burnt therefore, and three of his men drawne to Tiburne, and there hanged wrongfully.'[16]

15. Executions at Tyburn during the Elizabethan period.

Amidst the suffering there is the occasional irony such as that of the hangman being hanged: the entry for 2 July 1556 in Henry Machyn's diary tells us that on that day,

> 'rode in a cart 5 [persons] unto Tyborne; one was the hangman with the stumpe-leg for theft, the which he had hanged many a man and quartered many, and beheaded many a nobleman.....'[17]

Two of the regicides, those responsible for the death of Charles I in 1649, were executed on the Tyburn gallows:

16. The Triple Tree at Tyburn, c.1680. Note that the method of execution was by slow strangulation when the cart drove on. The coffins are in the cart.

Mr. *Francis Hacker*, and Mr. *Daniel Axtel*, were on *Friday* the 19th of *October*, about the same time of the morning, drawn on one Hurdle from Newgate to Tiburn, and there both Hanged; Mr. *Axtel* was Quartered, and returned back, and disposed as the former; but the Body of Mr. *Hacker* was, by his Majesties great favour, given entire to his Friends, and buried.[18]

Another prominent person who died at Tyburn, on 1 July 1681, was Oliver Plunkett, Archbishop of Armagh. Plunkett had been convicted of high treason for promoting Catholicism and sentenced to be hanged, drawn and quartered. One of the more remarkable consequences of this execution was that the various parts of his body travelled further after his death than they had ever done whilst he was alive. His remains were buried in two boxes in the churchyard of the nearby St. Giles-in-the-Fields, but two years later they were exhumed and parts sent to a Benedictine monastery near Hildesheim in Germany, whilst his head was sent in turn to Rome, Armagh, and finally in 1921 Drogheda. Though some body parts stayed in Germany, others were sent to Downside Abbey where they remain. Plunkett was canonised in 1975.

Other 18th-century reports illuminate the events at Tyburn:

6 May 1726 Last week one John Meth was committed to Newgate for felony: He is one of the persons, who two or three years ago was carried to the place of execution, and brought back and reprieved, by the lucky accident of having the Hangman arrested by the way; and being transported he quickly returned to England again, and took to his former trade; but will go near to verify the old proverb. (*London Journal*)

26 July 1729 Yesterday James Cluff was executed at Tyburn, for the murder of Mary Green at the Green Lettice in Holborn. He was to have been executed over-against the door where the murder was committed, but the neighbours petition'd against it. (*London Journal*)

12 June 1735 The criminals executed yesterday at Tyburn, as mentioned in our last, were pelted by the populace, and had dirt, &c. thrown at them whilst tied up to the gallows. Gregory, Sutton, and Hughes died without any signs of fear or concern; the former laught heartily just before he was turned off; Lewis was entirely stupified. As soon as they were dead, the bodies of Sutton and Lewis were delivered to their friends, that of Gregory sent to Edgeware to be hung in chains with his companions, and Hughes to be dissected in Surgeons Hall. Whilst they were hanging, a man attempted to pick a young gentleman's pocket of his watch; but being apprehended in the fact, he was hurried to a pond, where he underwent the usual discipline of the populace. (*The Old Whig*)

17. Dr Archibald Cameron drawn on a sledge on his way to execution at Tyburn. From an illustration of 1753. He was the last to suffer punishment in connection with the 1745 Scottish uprising.

A contemporary illustration depicts the unfortunate Dr. Archibald Cameron dragged on a sled from the Tower of London to Tyburn to be executed for High Treason. His crime was that of being on the wrong side in the 1745 Scottish uprising which culminated in the slaughter of the Scottish clans at the Battle of Culloden in 1746. The sentence on Cameron read as follows:

You Archibald Cameron, of Lochiel, in that part of Great Britain called Scotland, must be removed from hence to his Majesty's prison of the Tower of London, from whence you came, and on Thursday, the 7th of June next, your body to be drawn on a sledge to the place of execution, there to be hanged, but not till you are dead, – your bowels to be taken out, your body quartered, your head cut off, and affixed at the king's disposal, – and the Lord have mercy on your soul!"

Cameron's last days in the Tower are described in *The Newgate Calendar* which records that on the morning of his execution, his wife took her final leave 'attacked with fits, which left her only after grief had deprived her of her senses.' The *Calendar* relates the events at the scaffold:

'On the morning of the 7th June, 1753, the unhappy man was carried to Tyburn to be executed. He was dressed in a light-coloured coat, red waistcoat and breeches, and a new bag-wig. He looked much at the spectators in the houses and balconies, as well as those in the street, and bowed to several persons with whom he was acquainted. He was attended at the scaffold by a clergyman of the Church of England; and before his being turned off,[19] he declared that he was at peace with all men, and that he died firmly hoping for the forgiveness of his sins through the merits of his blessed Redeemer. When his body had hung during twenty minutes it was cut down, and the heart was taken out and burned, but the sentence was not further fulfilled. On the following Sunday, his remains were interred in a large vault in the Savoy Chapel.'[20]

The execution was of sufficient note that Horace Walpole (1717-1797), son of the prime

18. *The execution of Earl Ferrers at Tyburn for the murder of his steward, in 1760. For the unusual event of a nobleman going to the gallows, a grandstand has been built and there is a gathering of horseguards.*

minister Robert Walpole, commented that Cameron died with much dignity, and that the only matter of concern to the prisoner had been the ignominy of dying at Tyburn. He also observed that 'the crowd was so great, that a friend who attended him [Cameron] could not get away, but was forced to stay and behold the execution; but what will you say to the minister or priest who accompanied him? The wretch after taking leave, went into a landau where, not content with seeing the Doctor hanged, he let down the top of the landau for the better convenience of seeing him embowelled!'[21]

One of the most unusual Tyburn executions was that of Earl Ferrers (born 1720), executed in 1760 for the murder of his steward. Ferrers was sometimes an unpleasant, violent, half-mad drunk but there was no doubt that the killing was premeditated. In modern times he would probably have been declared insane and we are told that after his arrest and confinement in the Tower, 'his behaviour was decent and quiet, except that he would sometimes suddenly start, tear open his waistcoat, and use other gestures, which showed that his mind was disturbed.'[22]

His execution caused widespread comment and excitement, for it was unusual for members of the nobility to die on the gallows. Ferrers played his role to perfection. The *Newgate Calendar* reported that Ferrers was of a 'singular and most unhappy disposition' and a man who was of royal descent.[23] He was held in the Tower for two months, and then in April 1760 he was tried before the House of Lords, found guilty and sentenced to be hanged, followed by dissection. Execution was set for Monday the 5th May.

State Trials[24] relate that when it was time for Ferrers to leave for the sentence to be carried out, he sent a message to the sheriffs

> 'requesting their permission that he might go in his own landau, which was waiting for him in the Tower, instead of the mourning-coach which had been provided by his friends; which request being granted, his lordship, attended by the reverend Mr. Humphries, the chaplain of the Tower, entered into his landau, drawn by six horses, and was conducted in it, by the officers of the Tower, to the outward gate, and there delivered into the custody of the sheriffs, upon their giving the following receipt ...'

The 'receipt' requested for the still living Ferrers was, literally, just that. It reads:

19. Earl Ferrers in his coffin, before dissection and burial at St Pancras.

'*Tower-Hill, 5th May, 1760*
Received then of Charles Rainsford, esq. deputy-lieutenant of the Tower of London, the body of the within-named Laurence earl Ferrers, viscount Tamworth, delivered to us in obedience of the king's writ, of which the within is a true copy – Geo.Errington, Paul Vaillant, Sheriffs of London and Sheriff of Middlesex.'

The then extensive procession comprising 'a very large body of the constables for the county of Middlesex' got under way. The slowness of the procession brought forth the comment from his lordship 'that the apparatus of death, and the passing through such crowds of people, were ten times worse than death itself...'[25] When the procession reached 'that part of Holborn which is near Drury-lane, he [Ferrers] said he was thirsty, and should be glad of a glass of wine and water; but upon the sheriff's remonstrating to him, that a stop for that purpose would necessarily draw a greater crowd about him,' Ferrers acquiesced despite the lack of any future opportunity to enjoy a glass of wine and the procession continued. In an impressive display of calm and fortitude as the procession approached Tyburn Ferrers asked if he might stop awhile whilst he took leave of a friend he had spotted in the crowd. The Sheriff replied 'that if his lordship insisted upon it, it should be so; but that he wished his lordship, for his own sake, would decline it, lest the sight of a person, for whom he had such a regard, should unman him, and disarm him of the fortitude he possessed. To which his lordship, without the least hesitation, replied, Sir, if you think I am wrong, I submit....'

Ferrers' bravery and the nature of this public theatre continued when the earl's landau reached Tyburn:

'The landau being now advanced to the place of execution, his lordship alighted from it, and ascended upon the scaffold, which was covered with black baize, with the same composure and fortitude of mind he had enjoyed from the time he left the Tower; where, after a short stay, Mr.Humphries asked his lordship, if he chose to say prayers? Which he declined; but upon asking him, If he did not choose to join with him in the Lord's Prayer? He readily answered, He would, for he always thought it a very fine prayer; upon which they knelt down together upon two cushions, covered with black baize, and his lordship with an audible voice very devoutly repeated the Lord's Prayer, and afterwards, with great energy, the following ejaculations, O God, forgive me all my errors, - pardon all my sins. His lordship then rising, took his leave of the sheriffs and the chaplain; and after thanking them for their many civilities, he presented his watch to Mr. Sheriff Vaillant, which he desired his acceptance of; and signified his desire, That his body be buried at Breden or Stanton, in Leicestershire.'[26]

The moment had now come for Ferrers to depart this world, but he made a mistake when he summoned the executioner, to grant his forgiveness, and paid him five guineas. In the confusion he pressed the money into the hands of the executioner's assistant. An unseemly squabble between the executioner and his assistant then broke out which the sheriff put an end to. The final act now began:

'The executioner then proceeded to do his duty, to which his lordship, with great resignation submitted. His neckcloth being taken off, a white cap, which his lordship had brought in his pocket, being put upon his head, his arms secured by a black sash from incommoding himself, and the cord put round his neck, he advanced by three steps upon an elevation in the middle of the scaffold, where part of the floor had been raised about eighteen inches higher than the rest; and standing under the cross-beam which went over it, covered with black baize, he asked the executioner, Am I right? – Then the cap upon a signal given by the sheriff was drawn over his face and then, upon a signal given by the sheriff (for his lordship, upon being before asked, declined to give one himself) that part upon which he stood, instantly sunk down from beneath his feet, and left him entirely suspended; but not having sunk down so low as was designed, it was immediately pressed down, and levelled with the rest of the floor. For a few seconds his lordship made some struggles against the attacks of death, but was soon eased of all pain by the pressure of the executioner.

State Trials comments that whatever Ferrers' crime, by his behaviour during his final moments, he had earned tremendous honour:

'From the time of his lordship's ascending upon the scaffold, until his execution, was about eight minutes; during which his countenance did not change, nor his tongue faulter: The prospect of death did not at all shake the composure of his mind. Whatever were his lordship's failings, his behaviour in these last moments, which created a most awful and respectful silence amidst the numberless spectators, cannot but make a sensible impression upon every humane breast.'

The body was left to hang for the customary period of one hour before 'the coffin was raised up, with the greater decency to receive the body, and being deposited in the hearse, was conveyed by the sheriffs with the same procession to Surgeons' Hall near the Old Bailey to undergo the remainder of the sentence.' Where the *State Trials* leave off, the *Newgate Calendar* takes over and with great delight informs the reader that 'A large incision was made across the throat; the lower part of the belly was laid open, and the bowels taken away. It was afterwards publicly exposed to view in a room up one pair of stairs at the Hall; and on the evening of Thursday, the 8 of May, it was delivered to his friends for interment.'[27]

Ferrers was buried in St. Pancras churchyard in a grave dug to the depth, we are told, of '12 or 14 feet deep, under the belfry.' In 1782 the body was exhumed and reinterred in the family vault at Staunton Harold in Leicestershire.

Military Executions

In the area of what is now Speakers' Corner in Hyde Park a place was set aside for military executions and other punishments. The following two entries indicate the nature of the crimes for which soldiers were punished:

15 January 1726 Wednesday last three private Centinels of the Foot-Guards were whipt in Hyde-Park; one for desertion, another for being a Papist, and the third for cursing his Colonel; the last ran the gauntlet, and the others were ty'd to a tree. [*Weekly Journal, or The British Gazetteer*]

26 March 1726 Last Thursday John Ellis a private Centinel in Colonel Ingoldsby's Company, in the First Regiment of Foot Guards, was shot to death in Hyde-Park for desertion. About seven in the morning he was convey'd from the Savoy to the Tilt-Yard, and 10 men from each Company of the three Regiments being drawn up on the parade before ten; the drums beat the Grenadiers March, when the prisoner hand-cuff'd, and a clergyman with him, march'd on foot to the place of execution, when he seemingly died very penitent. [*Weekly Journal, or The British Gazetteer*]

Burial of Tyburn felons

What happened to the remains of executed felons? Marks devotes a whole chapter to this matter. Some probably found their way to a burial ground at Charterhouse. John Stow,[28] writing in 1598, records that Ralph Stratford, Bishop of London, purchased a piece of ground at Clerkenwell in 1348 which he enclosed with a brick wall.

'He there erected a small chapel, where masses were said for the repose of the dead, and named the place Pardon Churchyard. The plague still raging, Sir Walter de Manny, that brave knight whose deeds are so proudly and prominently blazoned in the pages of Froissart, purchased of the brethren of St. Bartholomew Spital a piece of ground contiguous to Pardon Churchyard, called the Spital Croft, which the good Bishop Stratford also consecrated. The two burial-grounds, afterwards united, were known as New Church Hawe.'[29]

This Pardon churchyard took executed felons and suicides – the latter were frequently given no burial in consecrated land and were interred at crossroads. There were two Pardon churchyards, one at Charterhouse, the one mentioned by Stow, the other near St. Paul's Cathedral. The *Grey Friars' Chronicle*[30] has an entry referring to the execution and burial there of 12 Lincolnshire men and reads as follows:

'*1537*. Also this yere the xxv. day of March the Lyncolnechere men that was with bishoppe Makerell was browte owte of Newgate un to the yelde-halle in roppys, and there had their jugment to be draune, hongyd, and heddyd and qwarterd, and soo was the xxix. of March after, the wych was on Maundy thursdaye, and all their qwarters with their heddes was burryd at Pardone church yerde in the frary.'[31]

At the Reformation the priory of St. John's was suppressed as was its cart used to transport deceased felons.

Death brought no guarantee of burial as we have seen in those cases where bodies went to anatomy instructors. A case without a specified date, but from the 16th century, was that of Awfield who was refused burial. His crime had been to distribute 'lewd and traitorous books.' His local parishioners refused a traitor to be buried '... where theire parents, wyeffs, children, kynred, maisters, and old neighbours did rest: and his carcase was retourned to the buryall grounde neere Tyborne ...'[32]

It is highly likely that those not sentenced to be hanged, drawn and quartered, then anatomised, or those that had friends to take their bodies away, were simply flung into pits in the immediate vicinity of the gallows. When a house was demolished early in the 19th century in the vicinity of the fixed gallows by Connaught Place and Uxbridge Road, an eye witness remembered 'quantities of human bones being found.' Further, as previously noted in the section on the location of the gallows, we are told by an 'old inhabitant' born around 1750 that 'I have every reason to believe that the space from the toll-house [on the junction of Edgware Road and Oxford Street] to Frederick Mews was used as a place of execution, and the bodies buried adjacent, for I have seen the remains disinterred when the square and adjoining streets were being built.'[33] A letter to the *Times* of 9 May 1860, from a gentleman who lived in Connaught Place at the south-west corner of the Edgware Road is reproduced at the top of p. 39.

Marks, relying on Challoner's *Memoirs of Missionary Priests*,[34] writes:

'We read of two priests and sixteen felons executed at the same time, in 1610, being all thrown together into a pit. The stories of bones found in the neighbourhood of the gallows may probably be

THE SITE OF TYBURN GALLOWS.

TO THE EDITOR OF THE TIMES.

Sir,—The site of Tyburn gallows has been a frequent subject of discussion among London antiquaries. It may be interesting to those who care for such questions to learn that yesterday, in the course of some excavations connected with the repair of a pipe in the roadway, close to the foot pavement along the garden of this house, at the extreme south-west angle of the Edgware-road, the workmen came upon numerous human bones. These were obviously the relics of the unhappy persons buried under the gallows.

I remain, Sir, yours faithfully,

A. J. B. BERESFORD HOPE.

Arklow-house Connaught-place, May 8.

referred to forgotten burial places or to pits into which, after a busy day's work, a score of bodies would be tumbled.'

An article in the *London Post* of 6-8 November 1700 reports: 'I am told, that 3 of the bodies of the condemned criminals executed, as mentioned in my last, yesterday at Tyburn, were begg'd, in order to be anatomized; that 3 more were put in coffins, and given to their friends, in order to be disposed of at their discretion; and that the other 2 were buried under Tyburn.'

We know that the bones of three of the Charles I regicides lie in the vicinity of the south-west corner of the Edgware Road, approximately where the Odeon Cinema Marble Arch is located. Pepys in his diary of Tuesday 4 December 1660 comments:

> 'This day the Parliament voted that the bodies of Oliver, Ireton, Bradshaw, &c., should be taken up out of their graves in the Abbey, and drawn to the gallows, and there hanged and buried under it: which (methinks) do trouble me that a man of so great courage as he was, should have that dishonour, though otherwise he might deserve it enough.'

The three, including Cromwell, were accordingly hanged and cut to pieces at Tyburn. Their heads were set up on poles outside Westminster Hall, but the remnants of their bodies were thrown into a pit at the foot of the gallows. The original site of Cromwell's burial

20. The statue of Cromwell outside Westminster Hall. There is irony here, since Cromwell ruled without a Parliament and, on the Restoration, his remains were exhumed and his head placed on top of a pole at the Hall.

in Westminster Abbey can still be seen and is marked "The Burial Place of Oliver Cromwell 1658-1661".

The Demise of Tyburn

The development of the area surrounding Tyburn and the opening of sufficient space in front of Newgate brought executions at Tyburn to a close in 1783. Even at this period it was seen by some as a break with tradition, and as such was unwelcome: Samuel Johnson observed to Sir William Scott that,

'The age is running mad after innovation; all the business of the world is to be done in a new way; men are to be hanged in a new way; Tyburn itself is not safe from the fury of innovation.' It having been argued that this was an improvement, –'No, Sir, (said he, eagerly,) it is NOT an improvement: they object that the old

21. Plaques on the wall of the Tyburn Convent at 8 Hyde Park Place reminding us of the Catholic martyrs who died on the gallows at Tyburn.

method drew together a number of spectators. Sir, executions are intended to draw spectators. If they do not draw spectators they don't answer their purpose. The old method was most satisfactory to all parties; the publick was gratified by a procession; the criminal was supported by it. Why is all this to be swept away?' Scott noted that 'I perfectly agree with Dr. Johnson upon this head, and am persuaded that executions now, the solemn procession being discontinued, have not nearly the effect which they formerly had. Magistrates both in London, and elsewhere, have, I am afraid, in this had too much regard to their own case.'[35]

Tyburn today

Little remains of the site of Tyburn but on the last Sunday of each April a walk takes place from the Old Bailey, on the site of Newgate Gaol, to the Tyburn Convent in Bayswater. The Convent is at 8 Hyde Park Place in the Bayswater Road, approximately 300 paces east of the presumed site of the gallows. At Tyburn Way in the middle of the Marble Arch roundabout is a reminder of the gallows which reads:

> 'For 600 years this crossroads was known as Tyburn. A plaque in the traffic island at the junction of Edgware Road and Bayswater Road marks the site where gallows were thought to have stood from 1571 to 1759. The gallows were known as the Tyburn Tree but were replaced by movable gallows when a toll-house was built on

the site for the turnpike road. In the 18th century Oxford Street was called Tyburn Road and Park Lane was Tyburn Lane. By around 1780 Oxford Street was fully built up as a residential area and the last public execution at Tyburn was held in 1783....'

The plaque, or roundel which marks the approximate location of the fixed gallows lies in a dangerous location on a traffic island between the Bayswater Road and Edgware Road, on the left. This more or less accords with the location depicted in the Rocque map of London 1746.

[1] A. Marks, *Tyburn Tree: its history and annals,* (Brown, Langham & Co. (London, 1908), p. 3

[2] *Ibid* p. 57

[3] *Ibid* p. 79

[4] *Ibid* p. 81

[5] *Ibid* p. 90. Marks' source is Matthew Paris, the *Chronica Majora,* which covers the period 1259 to 1422.

[6] *Ibid.* p. 61 The source referred to is Thompson, *Adæ Murimuth Continuatio Chronicarum. Robertus de Avesbury De Gestis mirabilibus Regis Edwardi Tertii.* Edited by Edward Maunde Thompson, p. 285

[7] Harleian Misc., iii.100-8, quoted from Marks

[8] This map is used in Camden's *Britannia*.

[9] Marks, p. 67

[10] *Ibid* p. 69

[11] Edward Walford, *Old and New London,* Volume 5 (1878), pp. 188-203.

[12] Marks, p. 70

[13] J.A. Sharpe, 'Last Dying Speeches: Religion, Ideology and Public Execution in Seventeenth-Century England.' *Past and Present,* No. 107. (May, 1985), pp. 144-167

[14] *Ibid*

[15] Matthew of Westminster, '*Flores Hist.*,' ed. Luard, iii. 134-5. See Marks, p. 101

[16] John Stow, *Survey of London* (1598), quoted in Marks, p. 105

[17] *Henry Machyn's Diaries,* (Camden Society edn, 1848) p. 109

[18] An Exact and Impartial Accompt of the Indictment, Arraignment, Tryal and Judgment (according to Law) of Twenty Nine Regicides, The Murtheres of His Late Sacred Majesty of Most Glorious memory. (London, Andrew Crook & Edward Powel, 1660)

[19] The expression 'turned off' was a common euphemism for the act of execution.

[20] The chapel is still in existence, and is in the Strand. It is open to visitors.

[21] Horace Walpole, *The letters of Horace Walpole.* (Bentley and Son, 1891), p. 341

[22] C. Pelham, *The Chronicles of Crime,* (1891), pp. 181-187

[23] *Ibid,* p. 184

[24] W. M. P. Cobbett, T. B. Howell, *et al.* (1809). *Cobbett's Complete Collection of State Trials and Proceedings for High Treason and other Crimes and Misdemeanors from the earliest period to the present time.* (R. Bagshaw: Longman & Co., London, 1809). Vol. XIX p. 501

[25] *Ibid* p. 502

[26] He was reinterred in the family vault at Staunton Harold in Leicestershire.

[27] *Newgate Chronicles* p. 187

[28] John Stow's famous *Survey of London* was published in 1598. It has been reprinted in a number of versions in modern times.

[29] Quoted in Walter Thornbury, *Old and New London,* Vol. 2 (1878), pp. 380-404.

[30] J. G. Nichols and Franciscans, *Chronicle of the Grey Friars of London,* London (1852). Volumes that describe political and religious events in London from the time of Richard I to that of Mary I.

[31] *Ibid.* vol 53, pp. 29-53.

[32] Marks, p. 50 quoting Ellis, 'Original Letters', 1824, ii. 298

[33] Edward Walford, vol. 5, pp. 188-203

[34] Marks, p. 51 quotes from Challoner's *Memoirs of Missionary Priests,* (1842), pt.ii. p. 37

[35] James Boswell, *Life of Johnson* (1791).

CHAPTER THREE

St Giles-in-the-Fields

St. Giles is a slightly run-down remnant of old London which lies in the immediate shadow of the Centre Point building in Charing Cross Road. The Angel public house and the notice in front of the adjoining church of St. Giles, rebuilt in 1733 on the site of two previous buildings, are reminders that this was the place of some of the cruellest executions to take place in London.

St. Giles was a rural place of execution, before being superseded by Tyburn. In the 17th century it had the first recorded case of sickness in the Great Plague of 1665, and by the 18th century the area was notorious as a rookery of slums, gin shops and brothels.

Its earlier isolation from the City is demonstrated in the wording of a 1541 Act ordering the 'western road' of London, from 'Holborne Bars' to St. Giles-in the-Fields, to be paved, 'as far as there was any habitation of both sides of the street'. The settlement of St. Giles had its ancient stone cross, which probably stood near what is now the north end of Endell Street.[1]

It is not known when executions first took place here but it is possible, as *Old and New London* suggests, that 'When criminals ceased to be executed at the Elms in Smithfield, or, as some say, at a much earlier date, a gallows was set up near the northwest corner of the wall of the hospital.'[2]

The hospital, for lepers, established by Queen Matilda *c.*1118, was in the immediate vicinity of the church. The first mention of an execution here dates from 1417 when Sir John Oldcastle, a member of the sect known as Lollards, which met nearby in the fields adjoining St. Giles Hospital, was hanged in chains over a slow fire. This is dealt with below.

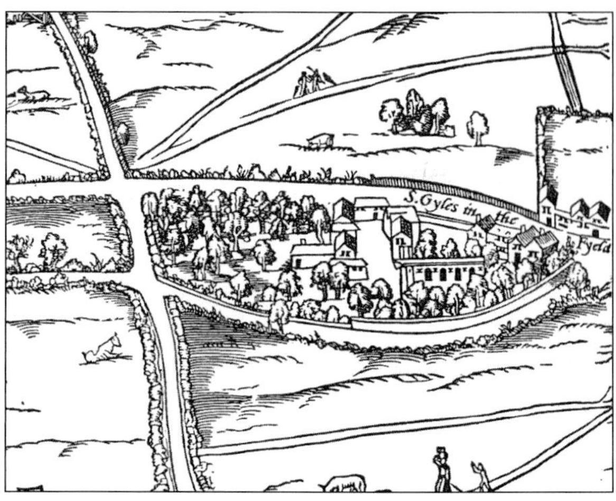

22. The settlement of St Giles-in-the-Fields on the 'Agas' map of c.1560.

After St. Giles ceased to be a place of execution its role in London's ritual of death continued. Being on the processional route from Newgate to Tyburn, the victims stopped at the 'Bowl' public house for their final glass of ale:

> '....it soon became a regular custom to present every malefactor, as he passed the hospital gate in the fatal cart on his way to the gallows, with a glass of ale. When the hospital was dissolved, the custom was still kept up; and there is scarcely an execution at "Tyburn Tree", recorded in the *Newgate Calendar* in which the fact is not mentioned that the culprit called at a public-house en route for a parting draught. The memory of this last drink given to criminals on their way is still preserved by Bowl Yard or Alley, on the south side of the High Street, "over against Dyott Street, now George Street" and Parton, in his *History of the Parish*, published in 1822, makes

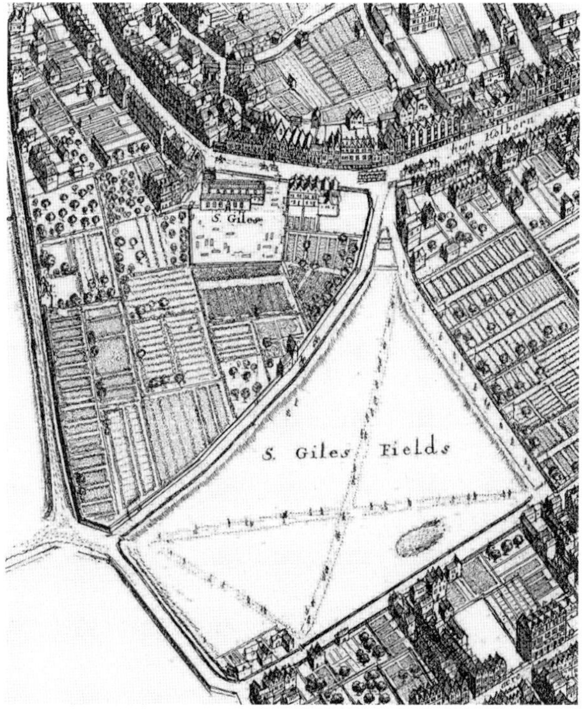

23. *St Giles-in-the-Fields in 1658.*

24. *The Angel, formerly The Bowl, where victims stopped for refreshment on their way to the Tyburn gallows.*

mention of a public-house bearing the sign of "The Bowl," which stood between the end of St. Giles's, High Street, and Hog Lane ... The "Bowl" would appear to have been succeeded by the "Angel," or to have had a rival in that inn. At all events, in 1873, the *City Press* reported that another memorial of ancient London was about to pass away, namely, the "Angel" Inn, at St. Giles's, the "half-way house" on the road to Tyburn – the house at which Jack Ketch and the criminal who was about to expiate his offence on the scaffold were wont to stop on their way to the gallows for a "last glass". Mr. W. T. Purkiss, the proprietor, however, was prevailed upon to stay the work of demolition for a time.'[3]

Location of the St. Giles Gallows

In the June 1856 edition of *The Gentleman's Magazine* a contributor noted that the site of the gallows at St. Giles in-the-Fields was 'near the north-west corner of the wall of Saint Giles's hospital, which was not far from the front entrance of the present church; it was removed to this spot early in the fifteenth century from the Elms in Smithfield.'

None of the early London maps depict these gallows, although the comment that they were 'not far from the front entrance of the present church' allows a close approximation of their position. When Oldcastle (Lord Cobham) was executed 'a new gallows was put up for that special occasion. But Lord Cobham was not the only distinguished person who here paid the last penalty of the law.' St. Giles' Pound was the execution place in the reign of Elizabeth I of some of the Babington Plot conspirators though Babington himself may have suffered at Lincoln's Inn Fields *(see chapter 10)*.

25. The church of St Giles-in-the-Fields, a print published in 1756.

26. The church of St Giles-in-the-Fields, 2007.

Executions at St. Giles

Sir John Oldcastle, or Lord Cobham, perished here in 1417 – the first execution we know of at this site. Cobham was accused of Lollardism, a political and religious movement inspired by John Wyclif, which sought the reformation and cleansing of the Catholic church. It was judged treasonable by Parliament, and Cobham was imprisoned in the Tower for his beliefs. He escaped, led an insurrection with the aim of capturing the king, but was once more arrested. He was brought to St. Giles from the Tower where he had been held on a hurdle, with his hands pinioned behind his back.

The historian Holinshed recorded that Cobham, an old man, 'much loved' was arrested, and literally dragged to his death to be hanged, and then burned for heresy. 'The brave old man was not to be taken without resistance. In the scuffle his leg was broken, and, thus maimed, he was laid upon a horse-litter, carried to London, and consigned to his former abode in the Tower.'

Parliament happened to be sitting at that time in London, and its records tell us the sequel. "On Tuesday, the 14th day of December [1417], and the 29th day of said Parliament, Sir John Oldcastle, of Cowling, in the county of Kent, knight [Lord Cobham], being outlawed (as is before mentioned) in the King's Bench, and excommunicated before by the Archbishop of Canterbury for heresy, was brought before the Lords, and having heard his said convictions, answered not thereto in his excuse. Upon which record and process it was judged that he should

27. 'The cruell Martyrdome of Sir John Oldcastle, Lord Cobham', in 1417, at St Giles-in-the-Fields.

be taken, as a traitor to the king and the realm; that he should be carried to the Tower of London, and from thence down through London, unto the new gallows in St. Giles without Temple Bar, and there be hanged, and burned hanging."[4]

On arriving at St Giles Oldcastle was assisted from the hurdle. He knelt down and offered prayers, as was customary, for the forgiveness of all, including his enemies. He then turned to the assembled crowds and warned them to obey the scriptures and the laws of God. Iron chains were then attached to his waist, and he was raised aloft and suspended over a fire, which gave Oldcastle an agonizingly slow death. He 'praised the name of the Lord so long as his life lasted,' but the clergy attending the execution forbade the crowd to pray for Oldcastle:

'The priests and friars stood by the while, forbidding the people to pray for one who, as he was departing "not in the obedience of their Pope", was about to be plunged into fiercer flames than those in which they beheld him consuming. The martyr, now near his end, lifting up his voice for the last time, commended his soul into the hands of God, and so departed hence most Christianly. Thus,' adds Holinshed, 'rested this valiant Christian knight, Sir John Oldcastle, under the Altar of God, which is Jesus Christ; among that godly company which, in the kingdom of patience, suffered great tribulation, with the death of their bodies, for his faithful word and testimony; abiding there with them

28. St Giles High Street in 2007.

the fulfilling of their whole number, and the full restoration of his elect.'[5]

In 1586 Anthony Babington and thirteen other Catholic conspirators were convicted of high treason for plotting the death of Queen Elizabeth. There is some uncertainty in the records as to whether Babington himself was executed at St. Giles or at Lincoln's Inn Fields, but the *State Trials* certainly places Babington at St Giles observing the demise of his fellow conspirators and the *Dictionary of National Biography* puts his execution at St Giles as well. Presuming that this was so, Babington was dragged on a hurdle from the Tower to the scaffold that had been erected for the occasion somewhere in the immediate vicinity of the entrance to St. Giles' church.

> 'Ballard was first executed. He was cut down and [disem]bowelled with great cruelty while he was alive. Babington beheld Ballard's Execution without being in the least daunted: whilst the rest turned away their faces, and fell to prayers upon their knees. Babington being taken down from the gallows alive too, and ready to be cut up, he cried aloud several times in Latin, "*Parce mihi, Domine Jesu!* Spare me, O Lord Jesus!" Savage [one of the conspirators] broke the rope, and fell down from the gallows, and was presently seized on by the executioner, his privities cut off, and his bowels taken out while he was alive. Barnwell, Titchbourne, Tilney and Abington were executed with equal cruelty.'[6]

The following day seven more of the prisoners were taken from the Tower to St. Giles. So cruel had been the previous events that Elizabeth ordered that the remaining conspirators should be allowed to remain hanging until they were dead.

What remains to be seen?

The main entrance of the present church marks the approximate location of the gallows, and there is a large notice by the railings in the churchyard which mentions some of the executions and the names of those that were buried in the churchyard. The Angel Public House, formerly The Bowl, is a few yards distant.

1 Edward Walford, *Old and New London*, Vol. 3 (1878), p. 198
2 *Ibid*, p. 200
3 *Ibid*, p. 200
4 Holinshed. vol. iii p.63
5 Quoted from the Holinshed Chronicles site at the Furness Library, University of Pennsylvania.
6 *State Trials*, p. 1158

CHAPTER FOUR

Newgate

An abominable sink of beastliness and corruption
Sir Stephen Jansen

Newgate Gaol throughout its 800-year history was renowned for all that was inhumane in early London society. It was a holding prison for those awaiting trial and punishment and in the manner of the lunatic asylum, Bedlam, was also a source of entertainment for the 18th-century upper classes, a place to visit and observe the inmates. After Tyburn gallows were abolished in 1783 public hangings continued at Newgate until 1868 when public executions were abolished altogether.

Diagonally opposite the site of the prison, in Giltspur Street, is St Sepulchre's Church. When executions were still at Tyburn, the condemned received nosegays outside the church, mounted a cart containing their own coffin, and began the

29. Detail from John Rocque's map of 1746, showing the Newgate Prison area.

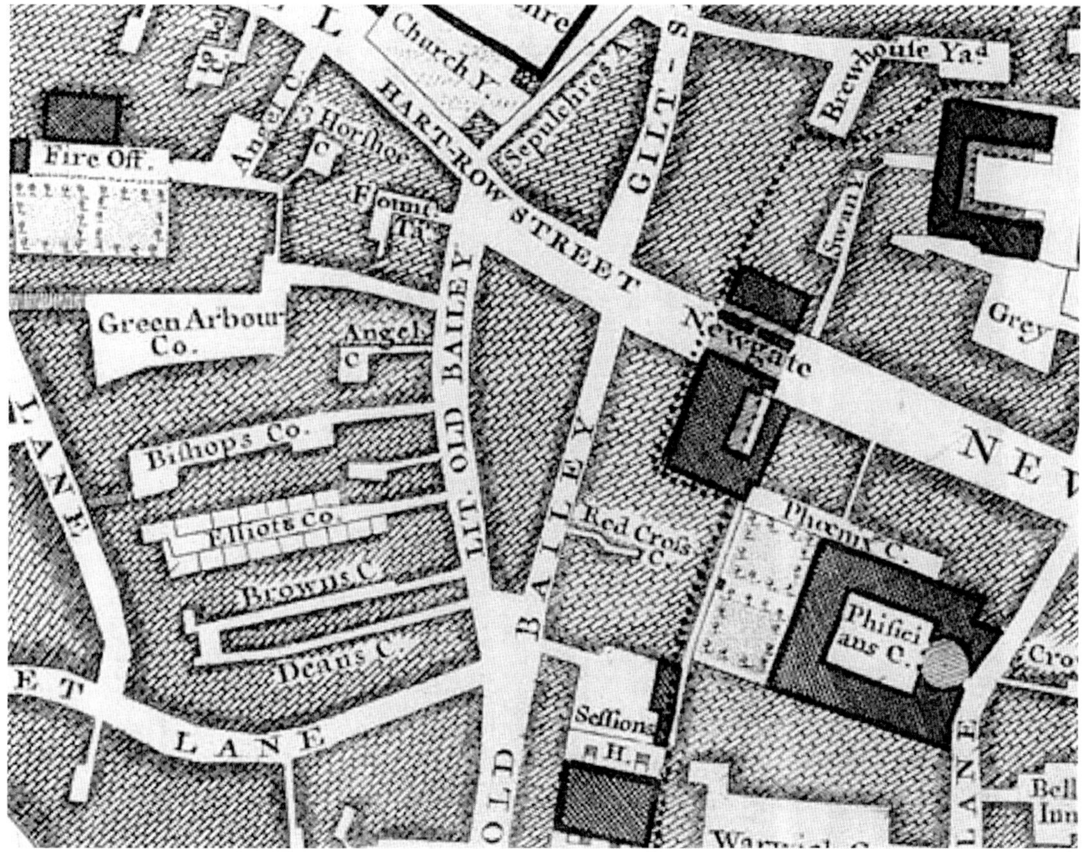

near three-mile journey to the scaffold. Sometimes the mob that travelled with the carts and lined the route would be so dense that the prisoners had to dismount and walk.

The gaol, which was closed in 1902 and demolished in 1904, was on the site of a Roman gateway, the remains of which were revealed when digging foundations for the Central Criminal Court early in the 20th century. As W. Eden Hooper in his 1909 volume, issued to mark the opening of the Old Bailey in 1907, says, 'the hundreds of years the abuses in the jail, the travesties of justice proceeding within the walls of the Sessions House ... have given thought to numberless humane persons.'[1] The prison was synonymous with squalor and corruption, from the jailers that charged prisoners for the necessities of life, to the conditions that meant that many who slept on filthy straw were more likely to die of disease than on the scaffold. Newgate served as a warning by parents to their children as to what could follow from a dishonest life.

Origins of Newgate

City Corporation records contain references to committals to Newgate dating from 1218. It is possible that a description *c.* 1188 by William Fitzstephen, clerk to Thomas Becket, refers to Newgate: He relates: 'On the west are two towers very strongly fortified with the high and great wall of the city, having seven double gates'. Stow in his 1598 *Survey of London* wrote: 'the next gate, on the west and by north, is termed Newgate, as latelier built than the rest, and is the fifth principal gate. This gate was first erected about the reign of Henry I. Or of King Stephen, upon this occasion.'[2] And then goes on:

> 'This gate hath of long time been a gaol, or prison for felons and trespassers, as appeareth by records in the reign of King John, and of other kings; amongst the which I find one testifying, that in the year 1218, the 3rd of King Henry III, the king writeth unto the sheriffs of London, commanding them to repair the gaol of Newgate for the safe keeping of his prisoners, promising that the charges laid out should be allowed unto them upon their account in the Exchequer.'[3]

Stow also tells us that in 1241 the Jews of Norwich 'were constrained to pay twenty thousand marks, at two terms in the year, or else be kept perpetual prisoners in Newgate', and that in 1326, Robert Baldock, the king's chancellor was put in Newgate. More tellingly, in regard to the appalling conditions and disease there, Stow says that in 1414, 'the gaolers of Newgate and Ludgate died, and prisoners in Newgate to the number of sixty-four'.[4] The prison's poor condition was a feature during its entire existence, as are references to bequests with which to sustain the inmates. From 1422 licence was granted to 'John Coventry, Jenken Carpenter, and William Grove, executors of Richard Whittington, to re-edify the gaol of Newgate, which they did with his goods.'[5] It was with Whittington's bequest that the prison was rebuilt, but if the intention was to improve conditions, it was a failure. The prison was destroyed in the Great Fire of 1666 and then rebuilt and extended in 1667.

In its early days Newgate housed a number of aristocratic prisoners. Stow records that in 1457 'a great fray' in the north between Sir Thomas Percie, Lord Egremont, and the Earl of Salisbury's sons led to many being maimed or killed. Lord Egremont was found guilty of having caused the 'fray' and as recompense was ordered to pay 'great sums of money' to the Earl of Salisbury. Until payment was paid, Egremont was committed to Newgate: 'Not long after, Sir Thomas Percie, Lord Egremont, and Sir Richard Percie his brother, being in Newgate, broke out of prison by night, and went to the king; the other prisoners took the leads of the gate, and defended it a long while against the sheriffs and all their officers, insomuch that they were forced to call more aid of the citizens, whereby they lastly subdued them, and laid them in irons: and this may suffice for Newgate.'[6]

The Horror of Newgate
Hooper quotes a pamphlet published in 1724 written by B.L. of Twickenham who 'had clearly spent some considerable time within the jail ...'[7]

'At the entrance to the prison was a lodge where prisoners are first received, and where they are fettered if the cause of their imprisonment require it."

Hooper notes that all prisoners were manacled unless 'a financial bargain' had been struck.

'These manacles were on both the hands and feet, and were heavily made. If it were known to the jailers that the prisoners had the control of money they were kept on until "easement" had been bought. If, on the other hand it was self-evident that the unfortunate person was penniless and without friends able to secure good treatment, he was either unchained or left manacled, at the humour of his jailers. Extortion was practised in Newgate quite up to the middle of the nineteenth century. Of course, by that period it had been so checked that jailers proceeded very cautiously, while, as more humane principles gradually ruled the prison, the pretences for extortion became less.'[8]

Worse than extortion was carried out in Newgate. Reinforcing an image of the place as an early chamber of horrors, the body parts of those that had been hanged, drawn and quartered were delivered to the gaol for post execution 'processing.' J. Ellwood, a former prisoner at Newgate writing in 1670, made the most gruesome of discoveries:

'When we first came into Newgate there lay (in a little by-place like a closet in the room where we lodged) the quartered bodies of three men who had been executed some days before for a real or pretended plot, and the reason why their quarters lay there so long was that the relatives were all that while petitioning to have leave to bury them; which at length, with much ado, was obtained for the quarters but not for the heads, which were ordered to be set up in some part of the City. I saw the heads when they were brought up to be boiled; the hangman fetched them in a dirty dust basket, out of some by-place, and setting them down among the felons he and they made sport with them. They took them by the hair, flouting, jeering, and laughing at them; and then, giving them ill-names, boxed them on the ears and cheeks. Which done the Hangman put them into his kettle, and parboiled them with Bay-salt and Cummin-seed, – that to keep them from putrefaction, and this to keep off the fowls from seizing on them. The whole sight (as well as that of the bloody quarters first, and this of the heads afterwards) was both frightful and loathsome and begat an abhorrence in my nature.'

In 1755 the Common Council reported to the Corporation that the gaol was 'incapable of any improvement or tolerable repair' and that it was overcrowded with victims of public justice, under the complicated distresses of poverty, nastiness, and disease. Hooper relates how in one of the many outbreaks of typhus in the prison (1750) that 'the Judges, the Recorder, the Lord Mayor, and others having business in the Court, to the number of over fifty, succumbed to the disease, and its ravages. Within the jail itself conditions were frightful. In 1767 Sir Stephen Jansen addressed to the Corporation a letter in which he described the prison as an "abominable sink of beastliness and corruption."'[9]

The prison was rebuilt by George Dance between 1770 and 1778, which probably explains why, when the philanthropist and social reformer, John Howard (1726-90), visited the prison in 1779, he found little to complain about:

'At my visit, in 1779, the gaol was clean, and free from offensive scents. On the felons' side there were only three sick, in one of the upper wards. An infirmary was building, near the condemned cells. Of the 141 felons, &c., there were ninety-one convicts and fines who had only the prison allowance of a penny loaf a day. Mr. Akerman generously contributed towards their relief. In the felons' court the table of fees, painted on a

30. A Condemned Cell at Newgate, in which three or four people could be kept. Dickens described them as stone dungeons.

board, was hung up.'

However, the prison was destroyed by fire the following year during the Gordon Riots though it was rebuilt by 1782.

New building or not, a Parliamentary Report of 1814 was damning of the conditions in the gaol. Referring to the duties of the prison chaplain:

> 'Beyond his attendance at chapel, and on those who are sentenced to death Dr. Ford feels but few duties to be attached to his office. He knows nothing of the state of morals in the prison; he never sees any of the prisoners in private. Though fourteen boys and girls from nine to thirteen years old were in Newgate in April last, he does not consider attention to them a point of his duty. He never knows that any have been sick till he gets a warning to attend their funeral; and does not go to the infirmary, for it is not in his instructions.
>
> The prisoners were allowed to drink and gamble, and their amusement was the repeating stories of past villany and debauchery.'

'I scruple not to affirm', Howard had said earlier, 'that half the robberies committed in and around London are planned in the prisons by that dreadful assemblage of criminals, and the number of idle people who visit them.' Those who refused to associate with the criminals were submitted to mock trial, in which the oldest thief acted as judge, with a towel, tied in knots on each side of his head, for a wig; and he had officers to put his sentences into execution. 'Garnish', 'footing', or 'chummage', was demanded of all new prisoners. "Pay, or strip", was the order; and the prisoner without money had to part with some of his clothes, to contribute towards the

31. Newgate Chapel in 1809, showing the death sermon being read to those about to be executed. Note the spectators in the gallery, and the coffin situated in front of the prisoners.

expense of a revel, the older prisoners adding something to the 'garnish' paid by the newcomer. The practice of the prisoners cooking their own food had not been long discontinued in 1818.[10]

Children often remained with their mothers in Newgate. It was reported 'that the condition of the children was too pitiful for words to convey. As one died its rags were snatched off to cover some still more naked form.'[11]

The Condemned and Newgate Chapel

A report by a Mr. Nield in 1812 describes the conditions of those awaiting execution and it is used by Hooper as the basis of his summary. The condemned cells were in the Press Yard and generally crowded as unless a prisoner had been convicted of murder, there could be a considerable delay in the carrying out of the sentence. Often prisoners had to wait for a final decision from the Secretary of State, as to whether the sentence would be carried out or commuted. In 1810 there were over 50 persons awaiting execution in the condemned cells, kept three or four together.

Once the confirmation of sentence had been received, in the form of a death warrant, the prisoners were fed on a diet of bread and water. Most executions were carried out on a Monday to give the condemned the dubious benefit of Sunday prayers in the prison chapel. Hooper tells us that 'this service was so obnoxious that many avoided it by denying faith. The condemned, often to the number of a dozen or more at a time, occupied an open pew in the centre of the chapel – in front of them being a table with a black coffin.'[12] Charles Dickens recorded a tour he made of Newgate[13] in 1836:

'The prison chapel is situated at the back of the governor's house: the latter having no windows looking into the interior of the prison. Whether the associations connected with the place – the knowledge that here a portion of the burial service is, on some dreadful occasions, performed over the quick and not upon the dead – cast over it a still more gloomy and sombre air than art has imparted to it, we know not, but its appearance is very striking. There is something in a silent and deserted place of worship, solemn and impressive at any time; and the very dissimilarity of this one from any we have been accustomed to, only enhances the impression. The meanness of its appointments – the bare and scanty pulpit, with the paltry painted pillars on either side – the women's gallery with its great heavy curtain – the men's with its unpainted benches and dingy front – the tottering little table at the altar, with the commandments on the wall above it, scarcely legible through lack of paint, and dust and damp – so unlike the velvet and gilding, the marble and wood, of a modern church – are strange and striking. There is one object, too, which rivets the attention and fascinates the gaze, and from which we may turn horror-stricken in vain, for the recollection of it will haunt us, waking and sleeping, for a long time afterwards. Immediately below the reading-desk, on the floor of the chapel, and forming the most conspicuous object in its little area, is THE CONDEMNED PEW; a huge black pen, in which the wretched people, who are singled out for death, are placed on the Sunday preceding their execution, in sight of all their fellow-prisoners, from many of whom they may have been separated but a week before, to hear prayers for their own souls, to join in the responses of their own burial service, and to listen to an address, warning their recent companions to take example by their fate, and urging themselves, while there is yet time – nearly four-and-twenty hours – to 'turn, and flee from the wrath to come!' Imagine what have been the feelings of the men whom that fearful pew has enclosed, and of whom, between the gallows and the knife, no mortal remnant may now remain! Think of the hopeless clinging to life to the last, and the wild despair, far exceeding in anguish the felon's death itself, by which they have heard the certainty of their speedy transmission to another world, with all their crimes upon their heads, rung into their ears by the officiating clergyman!'

Dickens refers to the custom of the condemned being forced to sit in the chapel, at prayer, with their own coffin beside them:

'At one time – and at no distant period either – the coffins of the men about to be executed, were placed in that pew, upon the seat by their side, during the whole service. It may seem incredible, but it is true. Let us hope that the increased spirit of civilisation and humanity which abolished this frightful and degrading custom, may extend itself to other usages equally barbarous; usages which have not even the plea of utility in their defence, as every year's experience has shown them to be more and more inefficacious.'

The Sunday prayers were often attended by curious onlookers who paid for seats in order to get a look at the condemned, and their demeanour whilst the ordinary uttered the prayers for the dead. A felon, Edward Wakefield, who was in March 1827 sentenced to three years' imprisonment in Newgate, left a disturbing description of what it was like to attend a Newgate chapel service for the condemned:

'... [the ordinary] talks for about ten minutes of crimes, punishment, bonds, shame, ignominy, sorrow, sufferings, wretchedness, pangs, childless parents, widows and helpless orphans, broken and contrite hearts, and death tomorrow morning for the benefit of society... [The thief] grasps the back of the pew; his legs give way, he utters a faint groan, and sinks to the floor. The hardened burglar moves not, nor does he speak; but his face is of ashy paleness ... the women set up a yell, which is mixed with a rustling noise, occasioned by the removal of those whose hysterics have ended in fainting ... This exhibition lasts for some minutes, and then the congregation disperses; the condemned returning to the cells ...'[14]

Amongst those sentenced to death were children. As late as 1833 a nine-year-old child who stole some paint from a shop, having poked a stick through the window, was sentenced to death. This was later commuted to detention in a penitentiary,[15] but before that, the child would have stood in front of a judge and with all the solemn paraphernalia of the law, would have been condemned to be hanged until dead.

The Condemned

Women sentenced to death were not segregated, and so mixed in appalling conditions with other women, and often their children, until they were taken away for execution. Their final hours were spent in one of the condemned cells. Dickens describes his visit to these and contemplates the horror of the prisoner's final hours:

> 'A few paces up the yard, and forming a continuation of the building, in which are the two rooms we have just quitted, lie the condemned cells ... all the prisoners under sentence of death are removed from the day-room at five o'clock in the afternoon, and locked up in these cells, where they are allowed a candle until ten o'clock; and here they remain until seven next morning. When the warrant for a prisoner's execution arrives, he is removed to the cells and confined in one of them until he leaves it for the scaffold. He is at liberty to walk in the yard; but, both in his walks and in his cell, he is constantly attended by a turnkey who never leaves him on any pretence.
>
> 'We entered the first cell. It was a stone dungeon, eight feet long by six wide, with a bench at the upper end, under which were a common rug, a bible, and prayer-book. An iron candlestick was fixed into the wall at the side; and a small high window in the back admitted as much air and light as could struggle in between a double row of heavy, crossed iron bars. It contained no other furniture of any description.'[16]

Attending an execution at Newgate

A description from 1827 by a person who was 'allowed behind the scenes' of an execution morning at Newgate gives us an idea of both the tension and mundane reality of the execution as viewed from within, in the company of the officials responsible for it:

'No further delay was allowed. The sheriffs moved on, the ordinary, the culprits, and the officers did the same; and that class of attendants to which I belonged followed. I shall not easily forget the circumstances of this brief, but melancholy progress. The faltering step – the deep-drawn sigh – the mingling exclamations of anguish and devotion which marked the advance of the victims – the deep tones of the reverend gentleman who now commenced reading a portion of the burial service, and the tolling of the prison bell, which, as we proceeded through some of the most dreary passages of the gaol, burst on the ear, rendered the whole spectacle impressive beyond description. Few steps sufficed to conduct us to the small room, or entrance-hall, into which the debtor's door opens, and from this we saw the ladder which the criminals were to ascend, and the scaffold on which they were to die. I was on the alert to detect any sudden emotion which this spectacle might cause, but could not perceive that it had the slightest effect. The minds of the sufferers had been so prepared, that a partial view of the machine to which they were being conducted, seemed to give no additional shock. No further pause was deemed necessary. The clock was striking eight, and the ordinary and the youth first brought to the press-room, immediately passed up the ladder. To the two culprits that remained, the gentleman whom I have already mentioned offered his services, and filled up with a prayer the little interval which elapsed, before the second was conducted to the platform.

I heard from without the murmur of awe, of expectation, and pity, which ran through the crowd in front of the prison, and stepping on a small erection to the left of the door, gained a momentary glimpse of a portion of the immense multitude, who, uncovered, and in breathless

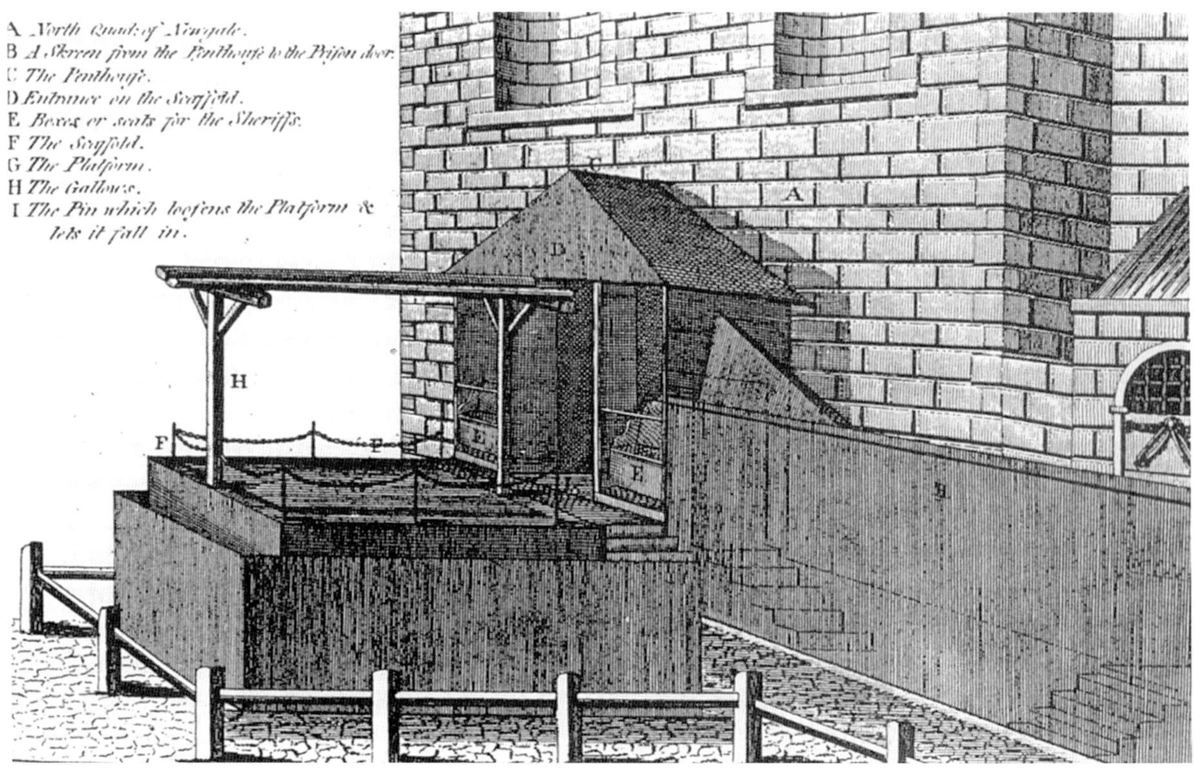

32. The gallows at Newgate.

33. On the first day of public executions at Newgate in 1783, ten people were hanged together on this portable gallows.

34. An execution at Newgate in front of the Debtors' Door, 1809.

silence, gazed on the operations of the executioners. I retreated just as the third halter had been adjusted. The finisher of the law was in the act of descending, when the under-sheriff addressed him –

"Is everything quite ready?"

"Yes, sir."

"Then take care and draw the bolt out smartly. Now, don't bungle it."

"No, sir - you may depend upon it," was the answer. And the obsequious anxiety of the hangman to seem polite and obliging, his apparent zeal to give satisfaction, though very natural seemed to me not a little curious.

Prayers, which had been interrupted for a moment, while the last awful ceremony was in progress, were resumed. As he read them, I saw the clergyman fix his eye on the executioner with a peculiar expression. He drew his handkerchief from his pocket, and passed it slightly over his upper lip. This was the fatal signal. A lumbering noise, occasioned by the falling of part of the apparatus, announced that it had been obeyed.

In that moment, a rush from the scaffold forced me from the door. The sheriffs, the under-sheriff, the ordinary, the gentleman who had assisted him in preparing the sufferers for eternity, and several other persons quitted the platform as expeditiously as possible, that they might not behold the final agonies of the unhappy men. Sir Thomas took me by the arm as he passed, and signified that he wished me to accompany him. I did so. Again I marched through the passages which I had recently traversed. Two minutes brought me to the door of the room to which I had first been conducted. Here my friend accosted me with his natural firmness of tone, which before had been considerably subdued by humane emotions, and said –

"You must breakfast with us."

I started at the unsentimental idea of eating the moment after quitting so awful a spectacle, as that which I have attempted to describe. But I had not sufficient energy to resist the good will which rather unceremoniously handed me in. Here I found the other sheriff, the ordinary, the under-sheriff, the city-marshal, and one or two of the individuals I had previously met, already seated.

They partook of breakfast whilst the victims hanged for the required period of one hour. Breakfast was pleasant and a sense of ordinariness and even humour prevailed which whilst taking part in the merriment and quips, the writer displayed an uncomfortable awareness of the awfulness of the events which had just taken place.' The visitor continues:

'I and the rest of the company laughing heartily ... The facetious sheriff now had it all his own way, and said several things, ... We were thus pleasantly engaged, when the aide-de-camp of the gallant officer in the blue and gold, – one of the city marshal's-men, entered to announce that it was past nine o'clock, and to ask if any of the company chose to see the bodies taken down.

"The bodies!" I repeated to myself, and the application of that word to those whom I had previously heard mentioned but by their names, recalled my thoughts which had somehow strayed from the business of the morning into unlooked-for cheerfulness, and presented, in that simple expression, an epitome of all that had moved my wonder, curiosity, and commiseration.

Again we passed through those parts of the prison which I had twice before traversed. We advanced with a quicker step than when following those whom we now expected to see brought to us. But with all the expedition we could use, on reaching the room from which the scaffold could be seen, we found the "bodies" already there. Nor was this, in my opinion, the least striking scene which the morning brought under my observation. The dead men were extended side by side, on the stone floor. The few persons present gazed on them in silence, duly impressed with the melancholy spectacle. But in this part of the building a copper is established, in which a portion of the provisions for its inmates is prepared. There was a savoury smell of soup, which we could not help inhaling while we gazed on death. The cooks too were in attendance, and though they, as became them, did all in their power to look decorously dismal, well as they managed their faces, they could not so divest themselves of their professional peculiarities, as not to awaken thoughts which involuntarily turned to ludicrous or festive scenes. Their very costume was at variance with the general gloom, and no sympathy could at once repress the jolly rotundity of their persons.[17]

Another account by Captain Shaw, a witness to one of the last executions outside Newgate in 1864, cuts through the often righteous, voyeuristic accounts common in the *Newgate Calendar*, and describes the events in the context of an awakening realisation that public executions were contrary to every precept of a country which believed in its own humanity. Hanging as a deterrent to crime can be seen to have little effect on those attending:[18]

'The scene on the night preceding a public execution afforded a study of the dark side of nature not to be obtained under any other circumstances. Here was to be seen the lowest scum of London densely packed together as far as the eye could see, and estimated by *The Times* at not less than 20,000. Across the entire front of Newgate heavy barricades of stout timber traversed the streets in every direction, erected as a precaution against the pressure of the crowd ... As the crowd increased wholesale highway robberies were of most frequent occurrence; and victims in the hands of some two or three desperate ruffians were as far from help as though divided by a continent from the battalions of police surrounding the scaffold.'

Shaw went on:

'The scene that met one's view on pulling up the windows ... and looking out on the black night sky and its blacker accompaniments baffles description. A surging mass, with here and there a flickering torch, rolled and roared before one; above this weird scene arose the voices of men and women shouting, singing, blaspheming, and, as the night advanced and the liquid gained firmer mastery, it seemed as if hell had delivered up its victims. To approach the window was a matter of danger; volleys of mud immediately saluted one, accompanied by more blaspheming and shouts of defiance. It was difficult to believe one was in the centre of a civilised capital that vaunted its religion and yet meted out justice in such a form.'

He captured the dark atmosphere that took place outside the building in the early hours of the morning of execution. At 4am workmen appeared,

'...immediately followed by a rumbling sound, and one realised that the scaffold was being dragged round. A grim, square, box-like apparatus was now distinctly visible, as it slowly backed against the debtors' door' [the door through which the condemned appeared was one storey above the pavement]. Lights now flickered about the scaffold – the workmen fixing the cross-beams and uprights. Every stroke of the hammer must have vibrated through the condemned cells, and warned the wakeful occupants that their time was nearly come.'

Shaw then described the activity that took place in and around the prison kitchen:

'Meanwhile, a little unpretending door was gently opened; this was the 'debtor's door', and led directly through the kitchen on to the scaffold. The kitchen on these occasions was turned into a temporary mausoleum and draped with tawdry black hangings, which concealed the pots and pans, and produced an effect supposed to be more in keeping with the solemn occasion.'

Shaw tells us that, almost as if taking part in a pre-rehearsed play, an 'old and decrepit man' made his appearance. This was the executioner, Calcraft,[19] who then proceeded to test the drop. By 7.30 am the street theatre was almost due to begin:

'The tolling of St Sepulchre's bell about 7.30 am announced the approach of the hour of execution; meanwhile a steady rain was falling, though without diminishing the ever-increasing crowd. As far as the eye could reach was a sea of human faces. Roofs, windows, church-rails, and empty vans – all were pressed into service, and tightly packed with human beings. The rain had made the drop slippery, and necessitated precautions on behalf of the living if not of those appointed to die, so sand was thrown over a portion. The sand was for the benefit of the 'ordinary', the minister of religion, who was to offer the dying consolation at 8 am, and breakfast at 9.'

Then came the procession of the condemned through the kitchen. Shaw describes the condemned as a 'cadaverous mob, securely pinioned, and literally as white as marble.':

'As they reached the platform a halt was necessary as each was placed one by one immediately under the hanging chains. At the end of these chains were hooks which were eventually attached to the hemp round the neck of each wretch. The concluding ceremonies did not take long, considering how feeble the aged hangman was. A white cap was first placed over every face, then the ankles were strapped together, and finally the fatal noose was put around every neck, and the end attached to the hooks ... The silence was now awful. One felt one's heart literally in one's mouth, and found oneself involuntarily saying, "They could be saved yet – yet – yet," and then a thud that vibrated through the street announced that the felons were launched into eternity.'

In the seconds and minutes after the trap was opened:

'One's eyes were glued to the spot and, fascinated by the awful sight, not a detail escaped one. Calcraft, meanwhile, apparently not satisfied with his handiwork, seized hold of one poor wretch's feet, and pressing on them for some seconds with all his weight, passed from one to another with hideous composure ...'

35. Execution Day at Newgate in the 1850s.

After the multitude had allowed the statutory hour to pass during which the bodies remained suspended Shaw informs us that the 'drunken again took up their ribald songs, conspicuous amongst which was one that had done duty pretty well through the night, and ended with "Calcraft, Calcraft, he's the man". The show was now almost over with the exception of the removal of the bodies. When St Sepulchre chimed 9 o'clock, 'Calcraft, rubbing his lips, again appeared, and, producing a clasp knife, proceeded to hug the various bodies in rotation with one arm whilst with the other he severed the several ropes. It required two slashes of the feeble old arm to complete this final ceremony, and then the heads fell with a flop on the old man's breast ...' Calcraft staggered under the weight and proceeded to 'jam' the bodies into their awaiting coffins.

Disposal of the bodies

At Newgate bodies were buried under paving stones within the jail: the same stones over which they had walked on their final journey to the gallows.

A visitor to the jail in the early 1860s describes what he refers to as the 'Burying Ground of the Murderers':

> 'On leaving the murderers' cells we followed the deputy governor through the midst of the convicts clad in dark-grey prison dress, consisting of jacket, vest and trowsers, and Scotch cap. At the farther end of the exercising ground we proceeded

36. William Calcraft, executioner.

37. Dead Men's Walk in 1902. Deceased felons were often buried beneath the stones of this passage.

through the corridor, and went under the covered arch, leading into an exercising-yard of the same description as the opposite side of the new wing. We continued our course until we reached the airing-yard attached to the female prison, which like the others, is covered with pavement, where we entered a long passage about eight feet wide, extending from the extremity of the associated rooms of the old prison, now to be used as an infirmary, to the nearest corner of the female wing, where it turns off in a right angle along the back of the female prison to the Sessions House adjoining. This portion contiguous to the female wing is the graveyard of the murderer; so that when conducted to and from the dock of the Old Bailey he passes over the ground which is to be his own grave. It is bounded on the one side by the lofty walls of the female prison, and on the other by a very high wall flanking it from the adjacent outlying dwellings. It is laid with pavement, portions of which have been displaced by the sinking of the ground, perhaps caused by the mouldering of the bodies beneath. Along the walls, on each side, are the initials of the surnames of the assassins, such as G for Greenacre, G for Good, M for Mullins, L for Lani. This plain looking passage is invested with tragic interest, when we think of the mouldering bones of the murderers rotting beneath, and carry our imagination back to the deeds of horror they transacted, the recital of which have brought paleness to many a cheek.'[20]

What is there is to see?

Of Newgate itself there are some remnants in much of the original brick of the Old Bailey. There are cells beneath the Viaduct pub almost opposite, and there is a plaque marking the site of the gaol on the wall of the Old Bailey itself. The Museum of London possesses cell doors belonging to the prison, whilst the debtors' door, in front of which the executions took place, is now in America.

In the immediate vicinity was until recently the Magpie and Stump public house at 18 Old Bailey, EC4 which stood on the site of an older pub of the same name. It once rented out its upstairs rooms to provide a grandstand view of the executions immediately opposite. Opposite now is a new development which has obliterated this once well known pub.

38. Newgate Prison in the 1890s, by then a remand prison.

St Sepulchre

St. Sepulchre-without-Newgate church, the ancient but much rebuilt church for Newgate prison, is close to the Old Bailey at the junction of Holborn Viaduct and Giltspur Street. It was from outside this church that the condemned began their journey to Tyburn in carts. It was also here that on 20 June 1698 the wall at the corner of the churchyard collapsed on the crowd who pushed too hard against it in their attempt to see six condemned criminals depart for Tyburn. A contemporary account in *The Post Man* gives one person as killed outright, four dying later, and 40 injured. St Sepulchre is the church named in the nursery rhyme 'Oranges and Lemons' as the 'bells of Old Bailey'.

On display in a glass case on a pillar at the south-east of the nave is the original execution bell, which from 1605 was rung at midnight outside the condemned cell. The clerk of St Sepulchre who traditionally rang the bell travelled from the church to the prison by way of an underground tunnel.

The church is open to the public Tuesday to Thursday, 12-2pm.

39. The Old Bailey, which supplanted the old prison. The buildings to the right are on the site of the Magpie and Stump at 18 Old Bailey.

40. *St Sepulchre's church, c. 1770.*

[1] William Eden Hooper, *The central criminal court of London, being a ... history of the court of Newgate and other jails ...* (1935 edn)

[2] John Stow, *Survey of London*, (1598, 2005 edn.) p.51

[3] *Ibid.* p. 52

[4] *Ibid.* p. 52

[5] *Ibid.* p. 52

[6] *Ibid.* p. 53

[7] Hooper, p. 26

[8] Hooper, p. 28

[9] Hooper, pp. 42-43

[10] Walter Thornbury, *Old and New London* Vol. 2 (1878), pp. 441-61

[11] *Ibid*

[12] Hooper, p.66

[13] Charles Dickens, *Sketches by Boz*, 'A Visit to Newgate', (1836) Ch. 25.

[14] Edward Wakefield, *Facts Relating to the Punishment of Death in the Metropolis* (1831), p.256.

[15] Hooper, p. 66

[16] Dickens, Ch. 25

[17] *The Mirror of Literature, Amusement, and Instruction*, Vol. 10, No. 271, Sep. 1, 1827, 'Behind the Scenes; or, a breakfast in Newgate'.

[18] Donald Shaw, *London in the sixties: (with a few digressions)*, (London, Everett, 1908), pp. 154-155

[19] Calcraft carried out between 450 and 500 executions all over England between 1829 and 1874. He was known for his 'short drops' which caused most of his victims to strangle slowly.

[20] Henry Mayhew and John Binny, *The Criminal Prisons of London and scenes of prison life.* (London, 1862). pp. 601-602

CHAPTER FIVE

The Banqueting House, Whitehall Palace
The Execution of Charles I

The execution of Charles in front of the Palace of Whitehall was one of the most significant events in English history. On the King's death, the monarchy was abolished and a republic, referred to as a Commonwealth, was created which held the country in a puritanical grip until the restoration of Charles II in 1660.

Unlike most of London's sites of executions, the scaffold placed outside the Palace in January 1649 was used only once. The site, enclosed on three sides, offered some security from a rebellious mob. Included here too in this description is detail of the events surrounding the nocturnal interment of the King in Windsor Castle on a snowy night in February, in the vault of Henry VIII and Jane Seymour. The interment was conducted with so little pomp that its location was almost immediately forgotten and was not established until the 19th century.

The King's road to the scaffold began at Carisbrooke Castle on the Isle of Wight, where he was held by Parliamentary forces from 13 November 1647. There is much on display at the castle connected to his stay there, and his subsequent execution. The chapel he prayed in is largely intact, and enough remains of this impressive building to capture the atmosphere of the times.

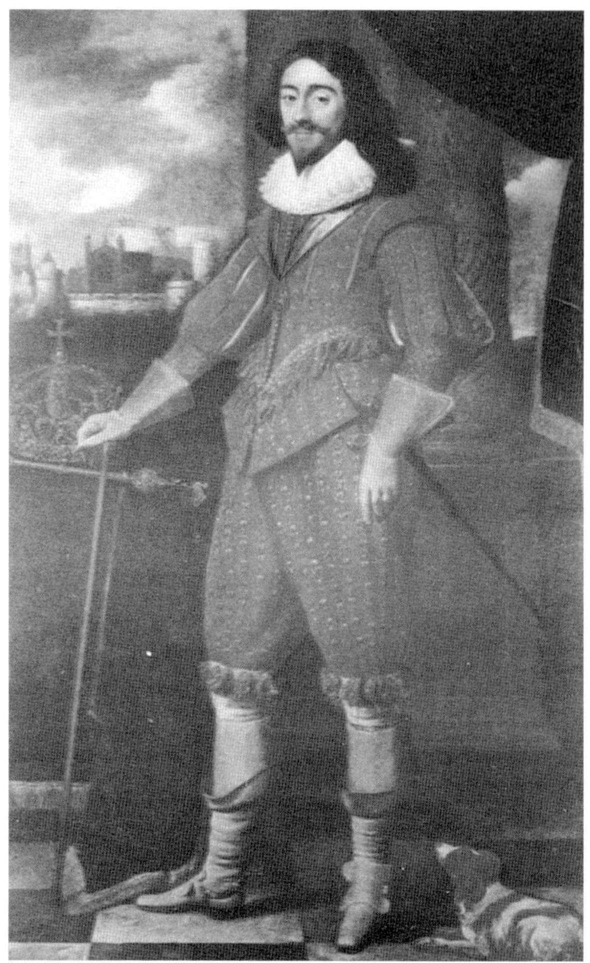

41. Charles I. Oil painting by Daniel Mytens, 1641.

In December 1648, shortly before his trial and execution, he was transferred for three weeks to the cold, damp and isolated Hurst Castle, a fort built in 1544 by Henry VIII on the coast near Milton-on-Sea. This is now open to the public. From here the King by way of Milford, Ringwood, Rumsey, Winchester, Alton, Farnham and

42. Carisbrooke Castle on the Isle of Wight contains numerous mementos of the King's incarceration, including the cap he wore on the night before his execution and part of a lace collar.

43. The bleak Hurst Castle on the edge of the New Forest where Charles I was held prior to being transferred to Windsor.

Bagshot, over a number of the days, was transferred once more, this time to Windsor Castle. He commented that 'Windsor was a place he ever delighted in, and would make amends for what at Hurst he had suffered.'[1] From here the King was moved to London for his trial.

The King's trial in Westminster Hall

The King's short trial in 1649 took place in Westminster Hall and ended on 27 January with 67 judges present. Charles entered into a long dispute with the court over the nature of his kingly power. He then launched into prophetic words that those present might in the years to come be called to account for the fate of the King. His words indicate that he was aware that he was likely to be condemned to death:

> 'It is an old sentence, that we should think on long before we resolve on great matters suddenly ... Therefore, Sir, I do say again, that I do put at your doors all the inconvenience of a hasty Sentence. I confess I have been here now I think this week, this day 8 days was the day I came here first. But a little delay of a day or two further may give peace, whereas a hasty judgment may bring on that trouble and perpetual inconvenience to the Kingdom that the child that is unborn may repent it,'

44. *The trial of Charles I in Westminster Hall.*

An argument then broke out between Charles and the President of the Court, with the King demanding to be allowed to refute the charges laid against him. The President responded that the Court had given the King 'too much liberty already, and admitted of too much delay ...' The President, after a lengthy attack on the the King, informed him that he should at least be penitent for his misdeeds. He then read the lengthy sentence which concluded with the words '... For all which Treasons and Crimes this Court doth adjudge, that he, the said Charles Stuart, as a Tyrant, Traitor, a Murderer, and public Enemy to the good people of this Nation shall be put to Death by severing of his head from his Body.'

After the sentence had been delivered, the death warrant which had been drawn up earlier, anticipating the 25th January as the date of execution, was given to three army officers to enforce. These officers included Colonel Hacker who retained the warrant until in 1660, as a prisoner in the Tower, he was ordered to surrender it to the House of Lords where it still remains. The instruction was:

'At the high Court of Justice for the trying and judging of Charles Steuart Kinge of England

45. *The Death Warrant of Charles I. Alterations and date changes on the warrant suggest that the date of execution was originally set for 25 January. It took place on 29th January, 1649.*

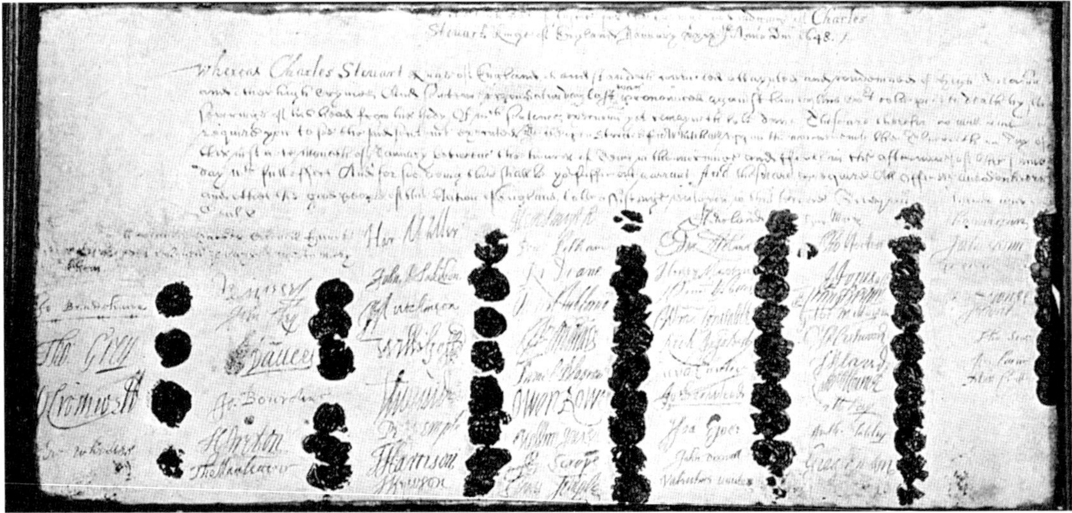

46. *The Banqueting House in the 18th century.*

47. *The Banqueting House in 2007*

January xxixth Anno Domini 1648.

Whereas Charles Steuart Kinge of England is and standeth convicted attainted and condemned of High Treason and other high Crymes, And sentence *upon Saturday last was* pronounced against him by this Court to be put to death by the severing of his head from his body Of which sentence execucion yet remayneth to be done, These are therefore to will and require you to see the said sentence executed *In the* open Streete before Whitehall upon the morrow, being the Thirtieth day of this instante moneth of January, between the hours of Tenn in the morning and *Five* in the afternoon of the same day with full effect And for soe doing this shall be your sufficient warrant And these are to require all Officers and Souldiers and other good people of this Nation of England to be assisting unto *you* in this service ...'

There were some practical considerations to be taken care of. Among other things a block and axe had to be put in place. On the day before the execution an order was issued

'that the officers of the ordinance within the Towre of London, or any other officer or officer of the store within the Towre of London, or any other officers within the said Towre in whose hands or custody the bright execution ax for the executing malifactors is, doe forthwith deliver unto Edward Dendy Esquir. Serient at Armes attending this court, or his deputie or deputies, the said axe, and for theire or either of theire soe doing, this shall be theire warrant.'

It is not possible now to determine the axe used but the late Robert Partridge in his detailed study of the execution comments,

'It is apparent ... that there was one special axe kept at the Tower of London which was used solely for judicial decapitations. In all probability, it was this axe which had been used to execute such notables as the Earl of Strafford in 1641 and Archbishop Laud in 1645 ... It is not possible to identify with any certainty the axe today as the Tower does not have any pre-Civil War inventories which distinguish an execution axe. The first inventory which makes this distinction is dated 1676. The heading axe now on display at the Tower has been identified using this inventory. Axes are particularly difficult to date, but this axe is usually identified as being of the sixteenth century and it may, therefore, be the very same "bright ax".[2]

Partridge points out that both the Earl of Holland, and Lord Capel, loyal followers of the King and executed shortly after him, asked the

48. Bishop Juxon (1582-1663). Oil painting by an unknown artist, c. 1640.

executioner if the axe being used was the one that beheaded the King, and were assured that it was.

Charles spent his final day at St. James's Palace putting his affairs in order. Thomas Herbert, who slept in the King's bedchamber and reported the events of the final hours, tells us that the King refused most visitors and was attended by Bishop Juxon who was himself regarded with deep suspicion by Parliament. Charles was allowed a meeting with his children Princess Elizabeth, 13, and Henry, Duke of Gloucester aged 8 who were being held by Parliament at Syon House, near Brentford. The rest of his family were abroad. In what was undoubtedly a distressing final meeting the king warned Henry that he must not allow himself to be made king 'so long as your brothers Charles and James do live for they will cut off your brothers' heads and cut off thy head too at last. And therefore I charge you, do not be made a King by them.' Henry, replied that he would 'be torn in pieces first', which pleased Charles. After the children left, the king turned away and walked into his bedchamber, and lay down on the bed, where from Juxon's description, the king's legs could be seen to be visibly trembling.

The king's final evening at St. James's Palace was spent with Juxon in prayer. At some stage of the evening Juxon departed having been requested to return the next morning. Herbert reported that 'for some hours his Majesty slept very soundly, for my part I was so full of anguish and grief that I took little rest. The King some hours before day, drew back his bed curtains to awaken me and could by the light of the wax lamp perceive me troubled in my sleep.'

When Juxon, on the next and final morning attempted to offer his condolences over his impending death, the king told him to 'leave off this ... We have not time for it. Let us think of our great work and prepare to meet that great God, to whom ere long I am to give an account of myself ...'

The Final Journey

The morning was cold and the Thames had frozen over. The King put on an extra shirt in case by shivering the observers took it to be fear. The two shirts survive: one at Windsor Castle, and the other in the Museum of London. Juxon and the King said prayers, and at around 10am Colonel Hacker came to fetch the King telling him that it was time to leave for Whitehall.

> '... the King, taking the Bishop by the hand proposed to go. Charles then walked out through the garden of the palace into the Park, where several companies of foot waited as his guard; and, attended by the Bishop on one side, and Colonel Tomlinson on the other, both bare-headed, he walked fast down the Park, sometimes cheerfully calling on the guard to "march apace". As he went along, he said he, "now went to strive for an heavenly crown, with less solicitude than he had often encouraged his soldiers to fight for an earthly diadem." At the end of the Park, the King went up the stairs leading to the long gallery, and so into the Cabinet Chamber of the Palace of Whitehall. '[3]

Herbert, who had walked with the King says that there were 'several Companies of Foot drawn up, who made a Guard on either side as the King passed, and a Guard of Halberdiers in company went some before, and othersome followed; and drums beat, and the noise was so great as one could hardly hear what another spoke.'[4] During the walk the King asked Tomlinson to allow the Duke of Richmond to attend to his burial. He would have seen the black covered scaffold and crowds as he approached Whitehall. It is believed he arrived at Whitehall shortly after 10am and was kept waiting for much of the day. He was offered food but initially refused it as he had already received the Sacrament. As time passed Juxon persuaded him to eat some bread and drink some claret. Much of the day was spent in praying. Herbert says they awaited Colonel Hacker's summons to the scaffold, '... mean time his majesty told Mr Herbert which satin nightcap he would use, which he provided. With the King at private prayer, Mr Herbert addressed himself to the Bishop [Juxon], and told him, the King had ordered him to have a white satin nightcap ready...'

Herbert says he felt unable to accompany the King onto the scaffold as he 'was not able to endure the sight of that violence they upon the scaffold would offer the King.'[5] Juxon offered to take the nightcap onto the scaffold and told Herbert to 'wait at the end of the Banquetting House, near the scaffold, to take care of the King's body ...' The delay was probably due to the difficulty in finding an executioner. Two men *(see below)* were found and at last before 2pm the King was finally called to the scaffold.

Colonel Hacker 'came ... to the bedchamber door, and gave his last signal; the Bishop and Mr Herbert, weeping, fell upon their knees, and the King gave them his hand to kiss, and helped the Bishop up, for he was aged ... Colonel Hacker attending still at the chamber door, the King took notice of it, and said, 'Open the door,' and bade Hacker go, he would follow. A guard was made all along the galleries and the Banquetting House; but behind the soldiers abundance of men and women crowded in, though with some peril to their persons, to behold the saddest sight England ever saw. And as his Majesty passed by, with a cheerful look, heard them pray for him, the soldiers not rebuking any of them; by their silence and dejected faces seeming afflicted rather than insulting.'

Herbert then makes an observation which has led to speculation as to exactly where from the interior of the Banqueting House the King stepped onto the scaffold: 'There was a passage broken through the wall, by which the King passed unto the scaffold.'[6]

The Execution

We have an account of the execution from John Rushworth, a committed Parliamentarian who served under General Fairfax, and who became secretary to Oliver Cromwell and was an eyewitness to many of the key events of the Civil War. He wrote a history of the era with a wrong-footed dedication to Cromwell's son, Richard. He tells us that on the day of the execution the scaffold was 'hung round with black' and that the axe and block had been placed in the middle of the scaffold. Ropes and staples were placed on the scaffold, so that should the King resist, he could be forcibly dragged onto the block. There was a 'cheap' six shilling coffin with a black velvet pall. The floor was liberally sprinkled with sand 'to soak up any blood and to prevent anyone from slipping after the execution had taken place.'[7] The scaffold was crowded. Among those present were Juxon, Colonel Hacker, and some shorthand writers who were there to take notes. Herbert, who was visibly distressed, remained in the Banqueting House. The King 'making a pass upon the scaffold' was concerned that the block itself was too low and asked if it would be possible to obtain a higher block. This was not possible. He then commented that as it would be difficult to be heard, he would make his speech to those gentlemen around him on the scaffold, which he proceeded to do proclaiming his innocence and the course of events which had brought him to the scaffold. The only matter he had on his conscience was

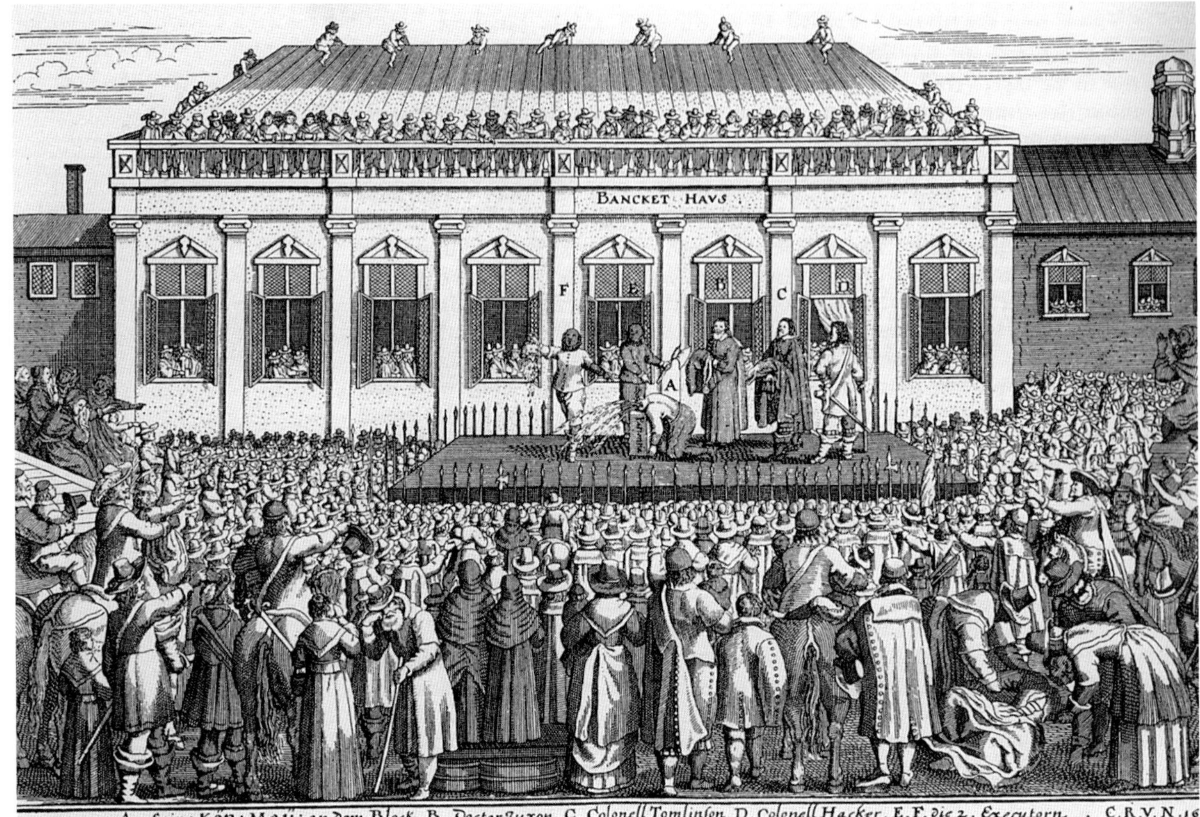

49. The execution of Charles I in 1649.

the 'unjust sentence' he had inflicted on the earl of Strafford, a similar punishment that he, the King was about to undergo. In the course of his speech we are told that he turned to a gentleman that touched the Axe, saying 'Hurt not the axe that may hurt me'. He then drew to a close by informing those around him on the scaffold that

> 'If I would have given way to an arbitrary way, for to have all laws changed according to the Power of the Sword, I needed not to have come here, and therefore I tell you ... that I am the Martyr of the people. In troth, Sirs, I should not hold you much longer, for I will only say this to you, that in truth I could have desired some little time longer, because that I would have put this that I have said in a little more order, and a little better digested, than I have done, and therefore, I hope you will excuse me. I have delivered my conscience, I pray, God that you take those courses that are best for the good of the Kingdom, and your own salvation.'

The closing act then began. Dr. Juxon was with Charles on the scaffold, and would have the task of taking care of the royal burial shortly afterwards. He prompted the King in what was required of him:

> *Dr Juxon* 'Will your Majesty, though it may be very well known your Majesty's affections to religion, yet it may be expected that you should say somewhat for the World's satisfaction in that particular.'
>
> *The King* 'I thank you very heartily my Lord, for that I had almost forgotten it. In troth Sirs, my conscience in Religion, I think is very well known to the world, and therefore I declare before you all, that I die a Christian according to the profession

of the Church of England as I found it left me by my Father, and this honest man (*meaning the Bishop*) I think will witness it.'

The King then told the surrounding officers that he believed he 'had a good cause and a gracious God' and that he would say no more. He then turned to Colonel Hacker and told him to 'take care that they do not put me to pain, and Sir, this and it please you ...' At this point the King's attention was distracted by a person on the scaffold again getting close to the executioner's axe. 'The King said, Take heed of the Axe, pray take heed of the Axe.'

Herbert continues:

'Then the King speaking to the Executioner, said, "I shall say but very short prayers, and then thrust out my hands.' Then the King called to Dr Juxon for his nightcap, and having put it on, he said to the Executioner, "Does my hair trouble you" Who desired him to put it all under his cap, which the King did accordingly by the help of the executioner, and the Bishop. Then the King turning to Dr Juxon, said, "I have a good cause and a gracious God on my side.'

Juxon replied that there was,

'but one stage more. This stage is turbulent and troublesome, it is a short one. But you may consider it will soon carry you a very great way, it will carry you from earth to heaven, and there you shall find to your great joy the prize. You haste to a crown of glory.'

The King 'I go from a corruptible to an incorruptible Crown, where no disturbance can be.'

Dr Juxon 'You are exchanged from a temporal to an eternal Crown, a good exchange.'

Then, according to Herbert, the King took off his cloak and his George, giving his George to Dr Juxon, saying, '"Remember." [it is thought for the Prince] and some other small ceremonies [were] past.' Herbert refers then to the King 'stooping down' and the Executioner striking. Another source is more expansive:

'Then he put off his doublet, and being in his waistcoat, he put on his cloak again; then looking upon the block, he said to the executioner, "You must set it fast."

Executioner. It is fast, Sir.

The King. When I put out my hands this way [stretching them out], then ... After that, having said two or three words to himself, as he stood with his hands and eyes lift up, immediately stooping down, he laid his neck upon the block. And then the executioner again putting his hair under his cap, the King, thinking he was going to strike, said, "Stay for the sign."

Executioner. Yes I will, and please your Majesty. – After a little pause, the King stretching forth his hands, the executioner at one blow severed his head from his body, and held it up and showed it to the people, saying, "Behold the head of a traitor!"[8]

A witness said that from the crowd came 'such a groan as I have never heard before, and desire I may never hear again.' The execution took place at a minute before 2pm. A witness, Sir William Dugdale, wrote in his diary of what followed:

'His head was thrown down by him that took it up. Bruised the face. His hair was cut off. Soldiers dipped their swords in his blood. Base language upon his dead body.'

The body was embalmed and placed in a coffin, probably the one placed on the scaffold. Herbert was waiting by the door in the Banqueting Hall for the king's body to be brought back. He reports that it was moved to the King's house at St. James's 'where was great pressing by all sorts of people to see the King, or where he was: A doleful spectacle! But few had leave to enter and behold it.'[9] The 'few' were those prepared to bribe the guards. Sir Purback Temple paid to be allowed to view the body and wrote that Axtell (as would Hacker, later to be tried and executed as regicides) was supervising the corpse and '... in a scoffing manner took me by the hand and said, "If thou thinkest there is any sanctity or holiness in it look here," where I saw the head of the blessed martyr'd King, lie in a coffin with his body, which smiled as perfectly as if it had been alive.'

The body remained at St James' Palace until Parliament gave an order allowing its burial. As Westminster Abbey was not permitted in case the tomb became a place of pilgrimage, St. George's Chapel at Windsor was agreed upon as a safe alternative.

Location of the Scaffold

A great deal has been written on the actual position of the scaffold that day. Lord Leicester's Journal of the time states that 'the scaffold was erected between Whitehall gate and the gallery leading to St. James's.'[10] Lilly asserted that it was erected 'just at the spot where the blood of a citizen had been shed at the commencement of the rebellion, when a mob were vociferating "No Bishop" under the windows at the palace, and some cavaliers sallied out to disperse them, and one was killed.'[11]

Nobody doubts that the deed took place on a platform adjoining the Banqueting House of Whitehall Palace. This building, designed by Inigo Jones, was rebuilt between 1619 and 1622 on the site of Queen Elizabeth's Banqueting House, which had been destroyed, together with the greater part of the ancient palace, by a fire in 1606. Sir Reginald Palgrave, an eminent 19th-century authority, quoted written evidence to the effect that the scaffold was built under the second or third window of Whitehall towards Charing Cross. His informant was Mr Thoms, Librarian to the House of Lords, who told him that some years previously he had been shown a stone which had been placed in the ground in front of the Banqueting House in order to mark the site of King Charles' execution. This is corroborated by a Mr Hugh Owen who saw the stone in position in 1931.

The King's funeral and burial at Windsor

Sir Thomas Herbert was responsible along with Bishop Juxon for the burial of the King, and he wrote an account of the events that took place in that cold February of 1649.

The king's body was 'embalmed and coffined, and those wrapped in lead, and covered with a new velvet-pall.'[12]

It was important for Parliament that his body was interred with minimum fuss and it was decided by his friends that it should lie in the Royal Chapel of St George since several of his royal predecessors were buried there, namely Henry VI, Edward IV and Henry VIII. Furthermore, Windsor Castle was a place that the King had always enjoyed. On 6 February Parliament authorised the burial there. The body was then transported from St. James's in a 'hearse covered with black velvet, drawn by six horses also covered with black; after which four coaches followed, two of them covered likewise with black cloth, in which were about a dozen gentlemen and others, most of them being such as had waited on his Majesty at Carisbrooke Castle and other places ...'[13] At Windsor the body was initially deposited in the Dean's House, which had been lined in black, before being moved to the King's former bedchamber.

The gentlemen concerned with burying the King then had the task of improvising a burial place. It is difficult to identify the chapel of today with a contemporary description of February 1649 which describes it at the time of interment as being 'so dismantled and ruined' that the mourners of the King 'recognised not where they were.' It was suggested that Charles be placed in the same vault as Henry VIII, but no one knew where that was, and it was argued that perhaps Henry VIII might not be an appropriate ancestor. Just as it had been decided that the King should be buried in the same vault as Edward IV, Herbert says:

> 'some noblemen came thither, namely the Duke of Richmond, the Marquis of Hertford, since Duke of Somerset, the Earl of Southampton, the Earl of Lindsey, Lord High-Chamberlain, with

Dr Juxon, Lord Bishop of London [Archbishop of Canterbury afterwards] who had leave to attend the King's body to his grave; and being fit to submit and leave the choice of the place of burial to those great persons, they in like manner, viewing the Tomb House, and the Choir, one of those Lords beating gently upon the pavement with his staff, perceived a hollow sound, and ordered the stones and earth thereunder to be removed, discovered a descent into a vault, where two coffins were laid near one another, the one very large of antique form, the other little, supposed to contain the bodies of King Henry VIII and Queen Jane Seymour, his third wife, and mother of King Edward VI of whom in the year 1537 she died in childbed ... the velvet-palls that were over them seem fresh, albeit laid there 130 years and upwards. The Lords agreeing that the King's body should there be interred (being about the middle of the Choir, over against the eleventh stall upon the sovereigns side) they gave order to have the King's name, and year he died, cut in lead, and whilst the workman was about, the Lords went out, and gave the Sexton order to lock the Chapel door, not suffering any to stay till further notice.'

50. Purported death mask of Charles I on a suit of armour in the armoury at Hatfield House. Courtesy of the Marquis of Salisbury.

In looking to clear the chapel of people except the workman, and lock the doors, it is probable that the Lords were attempting to stop relic hunters desecrating the body of the King. Intriguingly, they failed, but it was not the body of the king that suffered, but that of Henry VIII.

'The Sexton did his best to clear the Chapel; nevertheless (he said) a foot soldier had hid himself so as was not discerned, and being greedy of prey, got into the vault, and cut so much of the velvet-pall, as he judged would hardly be missed, and wimbled[14] a hole into the coffin that was largest, probably fancying there was something well worth his adventure. The Sexton, at his opening the door, espied the sacrilegious person, who being searched, a bone was also found about him, which, he said, he would haft a knife with.'[15]

The unceremonious burial of the King then commenced. The inscription on the coffin was simple, reading only 'KING CHARLES, 1648.[16] We are told that the King's body was taken from his bedchamber in the Castle to St George's Hall, where it remained for a short period and then taken the short distance to the chapel

'with a slow and solemn pace ... carried by gentlemen that were of some quality, and in mourning. The Lords in like habits followed the royal corpse. The Governor and several gentlemen and officers and attendants came after ... This is memorable, that at such time as the King's body was brought out of St. George's Hall; the sky was serene and clear, but presently it began to snow, and fell so fast, as by that time they came to the West end of the Royal Chapel, the black velvet-

51. A picture depicting Charles I with his head restitched to his body. It is not clear if this gruesome reconstruction is based on fact, but the king is shown here with dark hair whereas he had gone grey by the time of his execution. The three allegorical women represent England, Scotland and Wales.

pall was all white ... the colour of innocency ... being thick covered over with snow. So went the white King to his grave, in the 48th year of his age, and the 22nd year and 10th month of his reign.'[17]

Rediscovery of the King's Remains in 1813

From Lord Clarendon's account, as well as from Mr. Herbert's narrative of the interment of King Charles, it is to be inferred that the burial ceremony was a hasty one, performed in the presence of Parliament's loyal castle governor, who refused to allow the service according to the Book of Common Prayer to be used; and had hurried the ceremony in what was seen as an unseemly manner.

Immediately after the King's execution there were conspiracy theories regarding the fate of the King's body. After the King's death the chapel at Windsor was, as were many English churches, the victim of Puritan vandalism and suffered much destruction. For many years it was not even certain where the King's remains lay. Initially, Charles II planned that his father should be reinterred in Westminster Abbey, with a suitable monument, but although he often spoke of it, nothing came of the proposal. Many of those present at the interment had died, and those still alive went to the chapel to see if they could remember where the burial had taken place. They could not. It was not until 1813 when alterations were being made to the Tomb House in St George's Chapel that the location of Charles I's burial was again raised.

The building of a mausoleum in the tomb-house and the creation of a passage to it from under the choir of the chapel had accidentally led to an aperture being created in the side of the vault containing the remains of Henry VIII and

52. *St George's Chapel in Windsor Castle. The tomb of Charles I is beneath the middle of the choir. In the vault also are the remains of Henry VIII and Jane Seymour.*

Jane Seymour. Workmen then peered through the gap into the vault that should have contained two coffins, but noticed a third covered with a black velvet pall. A report was made to the Prince Regent, the future George IV, who felt 'that a doubtful point in history might be cleared up by opening this vault; and accordingly his Royal Highness ordered an examination to be made on the first convenient opportunity.'[18] The report by Herbert that the King's coffin had been laid to rest covered in such a pall made it a strong possibility that the third coffin was that of Charles. The exploration which then took place was carried out by the surgeon Sir Henry Halford, in the presence of some illustrious figures who included the Prince Regent himself, the Duke of Cumberland, Count Munster, and the Dean of

53. *St George's Chapel, Windsor, 2007.*

Windsor. Halford's report made a number of observations.

The vault was 'covered by an arch, half a brick in thickness' and was 'seven feet two inches in width ... and nine feet 6 inches in length, and four feet ten inches in height and is situated in the centre of the choir, opposite the eleventh knight's stall, on the sovereign's side ...' He observed that on the removal of the pall a plain lead coffin became visible with the inscription in large legible characters 'King Charles, 1648.' Upon a small square opening being made in the lid, just large enough to see inside it became clear that there was an internal wooden coffin, which was very decayed. Visible too was a body which had been,

> '... carefully wrapped up in cere-cloth, into the folds of which a quantity of unctuous or greasy matter, mixed with resin, as it seemed, had been melted, so as to exclude as effectually as possible the external air. The coffin was completely full; and from the tenacity of the cere-cloth, great difficulty was experienced in detaching it successfully from the parts which it enveloped. Wherever the unctuous matter had insinuated itself, the separation of the cere-cloth was easy;

54. A sketch of the vault at the second re-opening of the tomb in 1888. The coffin on the left is that of Charles I.

and when it came off, a correct impression of the features to which it had been applied was observed in the unctuous substance. At length the whole face was disengaged from its covering. The complexion of the skin of it was dark and discoloured. The forehead and temples had lost little or nothing of their muscular substance; the cartilage of the nose was gone; but the left eye, in the first moment of exposure, was open and full, though it vanished almost immediately: and the pointed beard, so characteristic of the period of the reign of King Charles, was perfect. The shape of the face was a long oval; many of the teeth remained; and the left ear in consequence of interposition of the unctuous matter between it and the cere-cloth, was found entire.'

It is clear from Halford's portrait of the contents of the coffin from the time that the face is unmistakably that of the King. Halford then detached the head from the body and held it up to view. His report observes that it did not seem to be attached to the body as

'... it was found to be loose ... and gave a greenish red (I have not asserted this liquid to be blood because I had not an opportunity of being sure that it was so, and I wished to record facts only, and not opinions: I believe it, however, to have been blood, in which the head rested. It gave to blotting paper and to a white handkerchief, such a colour as blood which has been kept for a length of time generally leaves behind it. Nobody present had doubt of its being blood; and it appears from Mr.Herbert's narrative, that the King was embalmed immediately after decapitation. It is probable that the large blood vessels, continued to empty themselves for some time afterwards. I am aware that some of the softer parts of the human body, and particularly the brain, undergo, in the course of time, decomposition, and will melt. A liquid, therefore, might be found after long interment, where solids only had been buried: the weight of the head, in this instance, gave no suspicion that the brain had lost its substance; and no moisture appeared in any other part of the coffin, as far as we could see, excepting at the back part of the head and neck), tinge to paper and to linen, which touched it.'

Halford then went on to describe the skull in relationship to the known features of the King:

'The back part of the scalp was entirely perfect, and had a remarkably fresh appearance; the pores of the skin being more distinct, as they usually are when soaked in moisture; and the tendons and ligaments of the neck were of considerable substance and firmness. The hair was thick at the back part of the head, and in appearance nearly black. A portion of it which has since been cleaned and fried is of a beautiful dark brown colour. That of the beard was redder brown. On the back part of the head it was not more than an inch in length, and had probably been cut so short for the convenience of the executioner, or perhaps by the piety of friends soon after death, in order to furnish memorials of the unhappy king.'

Halford then proceeded to describe his search for evidence of the executioner's work:

'On holding up the head, to examine the place of separation from the body, the muscles of the neck had evidently retracted themselves considerably; and the fourth cervical vertebra was found to be cut through its substance transversely, leaving the surfaces of the divided portions perfectly smooth and even, an appearance which could have been produced only by a heavy blow, inflicted with a very sharp instrument, and which furnished the last proof wanting to identify King Charles the First. After this examination of the head, which served every purpose in view, and without examining the body below the neck, it was immediately restored to its situation. The coffin was soldered up again and the vault closed.'

55. Sketch made by Sir Henry Halford of the King's head in 1813.

Whilst in the vault, Halford made note of the state of the two remaining coffins, those of Henry VIII, and Jane Seymour, and removed the fourth vertebrae of the king, the one through which the axe had cut, as a personal memento.

'Neither of the other coffins had any inscription upon them. The larger one, supposed on good grounds to contain the remains of King Henry VIII and measured six feet ten inches in length, and had been enclosed in an elm one or two inches in thickness; but this was decayed, and lay in small fragments near it. The leaden coffin appeared to have been beaten in by violence about the middle; and a considerable opening in that part of it exposed a mere skeleton of the King. Some beard remained upon the chin, but there was nothing to discriminate the personage contained

56. The nightcap said to have been worn by Charles I on the night before his execution. It is on display at Carisbrooke Castle.

57. A Royalist snuff box commemorating the King's death on display at Carisbrooke Castle. Note the image of the executioner's axe on the right.

in it. This would confirm the account of the soldier who entered the vault at the time of Charles's interment and stole a bone from Henry's coffin. The smaller coffin, that of Jane Seymour, 'was not touched; mere curiosity not being considered, by the Prince Regent, as a sufficient motive for disturbing these remains ... It may be right to add, that a very small mahogany coffin, covered with crimson velvet, containing the body of an infant, had been laid upon the pall which covered King Charles. This is known to have been a still-born child of the Princess George of Denmark, afterwards Queen Anne.'

The 'Executioner' Debate

Theories arose almost immediately as to the identity of the King's executioner. A note from the time in the Earl of Leicester's diary recorded that the executioners

'...were two, and disguised in sailors' clothes, with visards and peruques unknown: yet some have conceit that he that gave the stroke was one Colonel Fox, and the other Captain Joice, who took the King from Holmby; but that is not believed. This I heard for certain, that Gregory Brandon, the common hangman of London, refused absolutely to do it, and professed that he would be shot, or otherwise killed, rather than do it.'[19]

William Lilly, was examined before a parliamentary committee at that time, and gave the following information:

'The next Sunday but one after Charles the First was beheaded, Robert Spavin, Secretary unto Lieutenant-General Cromwell, invited himself to dine with me, and brought Anthony Peirson and several others along with him to dinner. Their principal discourse all dinner-time was only, who it was that beheaded the King. One said it was the common hangman; another, Hugh Peters; others were nominated, but none concluded. Robert Spavin, so soon as dinner was done, took me to the south window. Saith he, "These are all mistaken; they have not named the man that did the fact: it was Lieutenant-Colonel Joyce. I was in the room when he fitted himself for the work – stood behind him when he did it – when done went in again with him. There's no man knows this but my master [Cromwell], Commissary Ireton, and myself." "Doth not Mr. Rushworth know it?" said I. "No, he doth not," saith Spavin. The same thing Spavin since had often related to me when we were alone. Mr. Prynne did, with much civility, make a report hereof in the house.'

The *Newgate Calendar* opines that on the basis of some 'old accounts' it was most likely Richard Brandon, the common executioner who had carried out the deed.

'Brandon survived the death of the king but a very short time, having, as it was said, been seized with such severe compunction for being the instrument of the fatal deed, that he could never after look up and smile in the face of heaven.' He died on Wednesday the 20 June, 1649, five months after the execution.

The Sunday before Brandon's death, said the account in the *Calendar*,

'a young man of his acquaintance being to visit him, asked him how he did; and if he was not troubled in conscience, for cutting off the King's head. Brandon replied; yes, because he was at the King's trial, and heard the sentence denounced against him; who caused the said Brandon to make this solemn vow or protestation, viz. "Wishing God to perish his body and soul, if he ever appeared on the scaffold to do the act, or lift up his hand against him." And he further declared, that "he was no sooner on the scaffold (to do that wicked act) but he immediately felt a trembling, and ever since, to his death, continued in the like agony ... He likewise confessed, that he had thirty pounds for his pains, and all paid him in half crowns, within an hour after the fatal blow was struck, and that he took an orange stuck full of cloves, and a handkerchief, out of the King's coat-pocket. As soon as he had descended from the scaffold, he was proffered twenty shillings for that orange, by a gentleman in Whitehall, but he refused the same, and afterwards sold it for ten shillings in Rosemary-lane.

The *Calendar* continues:

'About six o'clock that evening, he returned to his wife, living in Rosemary-lane, and gave her the money, saying, it was the dearest money he ever earned in his life, which prophetical words were soon made manifest. About three days before his death, he lay speechless, uttering many a sigh and heavy groan, and in a most deplorable manner departed his bed of sorrow.

For his burial, great store of wine was sent by the sheriffs of the city of London, and a great multitude of people stood waiting, to see his corpse carried to the church-yard; some crying out, hang him, the rogue, bury him in a dung-hill; others pressed upon the coffin, saying, "they would quarter him, for executing the King"; insomuch that the church-wardens and overseers were fain to come for the suppressing them, and with great difficulty he was at last carried to Whitechapel church-yard, having a bunch of rosemary at the end of the coffin, and on the top thereof, a rope, tied across, from one end to the other.'

The burial Register for Whitechapel has an entry under 1649:

'June 21st, Richard Brandon, a man out of Rosemary Lane. This R. Brandon is supposed to have cut off the head of Charles the First.'

Geoffrey Robertson QC in an article for *History Today*[20] believes that it is likely to have been Brandon because when he was being taken across the Thames shortly after the execution, by a bargeman who recognised him, he was trembling. Further still, Brandon had been escorted to the barge by soldiers whom he tipped with a gold half crown ... the executioner had been paid in half crowns. Tipping the soldiers suggested that he was grateful to the soldiers for escorting him away from the scene safely. Robertson also says that suggestions that certain

58. The bust and tablet over the door of the entrance to the Banqueting House in Whitehall.

parliamentary soldiers had carried out the execution were unlikely as the king had been executed in an expert manner. It was, however, likely that Cromwell had arranged backup in case Brandon had refused to undertake the task, and this was where the rumours and subsequent accusations had come from.

What remains to be seen?

For the dedicated follower of the fate of Charles I, the journey should begin at Carisbrooke Castle on the Isle of Wight, easily accessible by ferry from Southampton, and impressive enough to withstand a full day's tourism. The castle, an imposing, atmospheric building, partly in ruins, is not far from Newport. The chamber where the King stayed is preserved as Charles may have known it, and numerous relics relating to Charles and the royal family of the time are on display including gifts from the King to members of the Carisbrooke staff.

Westminster Hall, the scene of the trial, can be visited, but is subject to strict security restrictions. The Banqueting House publishes opening times but can be closed without notice when functions take place. The Museum of London has one of the shirts in which Charles was executed, suitably stained. A recent attempt to confirm these stains as being the blood of the king proved inconclusive.

At the northern end of Whitehall, south of Trafalgar Square, is the equestrian statue of Charles I. It has had a complex history. Privately commissioned by Lord Weston, it was sculpted by Hubert le Sueur and cast in 1633, sixteen years *before* the King's death. It was first erected in Weston's garden at Roehampton. The owner of Weston's estate at the end of the first Civil War was Sir Thomas Dawes and as he was adjudged

59. The plaque in the above picture.

'delinquent', the house and grounds were taken by the Parliamentary authorities and the statue was sold for £150 to the parish of St Paul's Covent Garden to ornament their churchyard. In 1650, during the second Civil War, the destruction of royal statues was ordered. At the Restoration in 1660 a Holborn brazier, John Brazier, testified that he had bought the statue from St Paul's Covent Garden as scrap and had been asked by the Parliamentary authorities to destroy it. He had, however, concealed it instead 'with great hazard, charge and care, preserving it under ground'. In 1675 the statue was bought by Charles II and erected in its present, and appropriate, location. Each year, on the anniversary of the King's death, the statue is the focus of a ceremony dedicated to the King's memory.

1 T.S.B. Herbert, *The Trial of Charles I. A contemporary account taken from the memoirs of Sir T. Herbert and John Rushworth.* Edited by Roger Lockyer *et al.* (London, Folio Society,1959) p. 59

2 R. B. Partridge, *'O horrable murder': the trial, execution and burial of King Charles I.* (London, Rubicon, 1998), p. 77

3 *The trials of Charles the First, and of some of the regicides : with biographies of Bradshaw, Ireton, Harrison, and others,* (Murray, 1839), p. 104

4 Herbert, p. 129

5 *Ibid* p. 130

6 *Ibid* p. 130

7 John Rushworth (*c.*1612-1690) was a messenger between King and Parliament and recorded events first hand referred to as the 'Historical Collections'.

8 Partridge, p. 94

9 Herbert, pp 141-142

10 *Ibid*

11 *Ibid* p. 106

12 *Ibid* p. 142

13 *Ibid* p.143

14 Made a hole with a gimlet

15 Herbert, p. 145

16 Old style year dating. New style is 1649

17 Herbert, p.146

18 Sir Henry Halford's Report To The Prince Regent, in 1813, on the Discovery and Examination of the Body of King Charles I in St. George's Chapel, Windsor.

19 From the Earl of Leicester's Diary, Sydney Papers, pp. 61 and 183 taken from J. W. Clayton, *Personal memoirs of Charles the Second: with sketches of his court and times.* (London, Charles J. Skeet, 1859).

20 Geoffrey Robertson QC, 'Who Killed the King?' in *History Today. Nov. 2006,* pp. 58-59

CHAPTER SIX

Charing Cross

There are a number of references to a gallows at Charing Cross. The Braun and Hogenberg map of London of *c*.1560 depicts gallows almost directly in front of today's National Gallery to the south of Nelson's Column.

Henry Machyn, a funeral director who kept a diary of London events between 1550 and 1563, makes frequent reference to executions at Charing Cross.

'The 25th day of October [1554] was hanged at Charing Cross a Spaniard who killed a servant of Sir George Gifford, the which was slain with-out Temple Bar.'[1]

'The 26th day of April [1555] was carried from the Marshalsea [Prison] in a cart through London unto Charing Cross to the gallows, and there hanged three men for robbing of certain Spaniards of treasure of gold out of the abbey of Westminster.'

He continues:

'The 29th day of April was cut down off the gallows a man that was hanged the 26th day of April, a poulter's servant that was one of them that did robbed the Spaniard within-in Westminster Abbey, and he hanged in a gown of tawny fryse and a doublet of tawny taffeta and a pair of fine hose lined with sarsenet, and after buried under the gallows, rayllyng against the pope and the mass, and hanged 4 days.'

There was to be no peace for the poulterer's assistant:

'The 7th day of May was taken out of his grave the same man that was buried beside the gallows at Charing Cross, a poulterer, and burned beside the gallows.' [2]

John Selman, a cutpurse, captured the popular imagination of early 17th-century London. He

60. A pamphlet devoted to the arraignment of John Selman, accused of theft in the King's Chapel. He was executed at Charing Cross in 1612.

THE ARAIGNMENT
of *Iohn Selman*, who was executed
neere Charing-Crosse the 7.of Ianuary, 1612.for
a Fellony by him committed in the Kings Chappell
at White-Hall vpon Christmas day last, in presence
of the King and diuers of the Nobility.

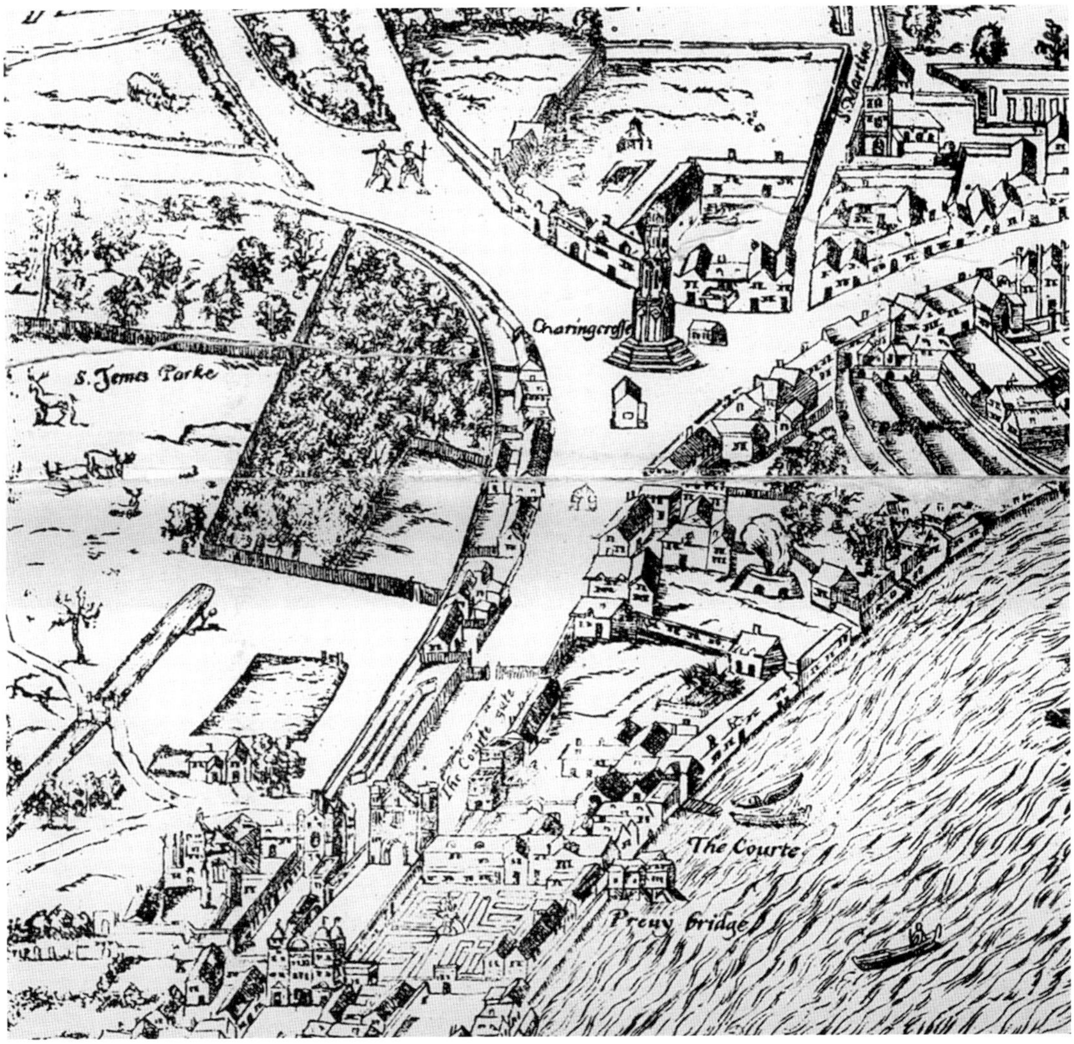

61. *Charing Cross on the 'Agas' map of c.1560, with Whitehall to the south. The gallows were just south of the Eleanor Cross (erected c.1296, demolished 1647). The word Charing denotes a bend in the river (Thames) here.*

impersonated a 'gentleman' to enter the royal chapel at Whitehall, where, on Christmas Day, in the presence of King James I, he picked a pocket, and found himself, but posthumously, celebrated in a number broadsheets and ballads of the time. The most authentic account of the events comes from an anonymous pamphlet in which we are told that Selman

> 'did presume to come into the Chappell at White-Hall, with intent and purpose ... either to cut a purse or pick a pocket ... in very good and seemely apparell, like unto a Gentleman, or Citizen: *viz.* a faire blacke Cloake laced, and either lined thorow or faced with velvet. The rest of his apparel in reasonable maner being answerable thereunto. Which was the cause that he without resistance had free entrance into that holy and sanctified place'. A witness, Edmund Doubleday, recognized Selman because 'at Westminster Hall in the Cheker Chamber ... [he] was very neere about me, ... having no businesse with me ... [which] made me

very strickly, but covertly to watch him, notwithstanding his formality in apparrell'

Selman, 'after long hawking, and following,' picked the pocket of a servant to Lord Harrington of Exton, and left the chapel. Doubleday quickly alerted the servant; they both followed and apprehended Selman. On searching him they found Barry's purse containing 40s. Their 'hasty following of Selman forth of the Chappell, caused the by-standers with admiration to look after them, and one to enquire of another, what might bee the cause of that sodaine tumult. In briefe it came to his Maiesties eare, who being then in his royall person [with his family and court] ... ready to receive the Sacrament, was somewhat disturbed with the report thereof, ... [and] gave commandement that the malefactor should be detained and further examined.'

Selman was then brought before Sir Robert Bannister, a Household official, and having been caught red-handed, had little choice but to confess the crime. He was then taken to the Marshalsea Prison, and put back into the clothing seen as more appropriate to his lower class status. At his trial, he was condemned to death and begged that his wife be allowed to take his body and give it a Christian burial. The judge was Sir Francis Bacon, who agreed that if Selman identified fellow cut-purses he would allow his request. The time needed bought Selman a short reprieve as the execution was postponed until immediately after Christmas. It was to take place between Whitehall and Charing Cross, but not at the court gate.

'The Dying Speech of John Selman *at his place of execution, Charing Cross, on 7 January 1612*

I am come (as you see) patiently to offer up the sweet, and dear sacrifice of my life, a life, which I have gracelessly abused, and by the unruly course thereof, made my death a scandal to my kindred and acquaintance: I have consumed fortune's gifts in riotous companies, wasted my good name in the purchase of goods unlawfully gotten, and now ending my days in too late repentance, I am placed in the rank of reprobates, which the rusty canker of time must needs turn to oblivion. I stand here as shame's example, ready to be spewed out of the Commonwealth. I confess I have known too much, performed more, but consented to most: I have been the only corruption of many ripe witted youth, and leader of them to confusion. Pardon me God, for that is now a burden to my conscience, wash it away sweet Creator, that I may spotless enter into thy glorious kingdom. Whereupon being demanded, if he would discover any of his fraternity, for the good of the Commonwealth or not: Answered, that he had already left the names of divers notorious malefactors in writing behind him, which he thought sufficient. So he requested the quietness of conscience that his soul might depart without molestation. For (quoth he) I have deserved death long before this time, and deservedly now I suffer death. The offense I die for, was high presumption, a fact done even in the Kings Majesty's presence, even in the Church of God, in the time of divine Service, and the celebration of the Sacred Communion, for which if forgiveness may descend from God's tribunal Throne, with penitence of heart I desire it, all which being spoken, he patiently left this world for another life ...'

In the annals of executions Charing Cross is best known as being the place of death for the regicides who had signed the death warrant of Charles I in 1649. Charing Cross was appropriately close to the Banqueting House in Whitehall, where the king had died, and the present statue of Charles I on horseback marks the spot where the unfortunates met their own deaths.

Execution of Thomas Harrison, regicide

Major-General Thomas Harrison was eminent in the execution of Charles I and was responsible for bringing the King from captivity at Hurst Castle to trial in London. He was also a signatory to the King's death warrant. In order to restore confidence and heal a divided country, Charles II on his return in 1660 issued an amnesty known as the Declaration of Breda, outlining the

62. *Thomas Harrison, regicide.*

conditions in which he would return to the throne. He declared that:

> '... we do grant a free and general pardon ... to all our subjects, of what degree or quality so ever, who, within forty days after the publishing hereof, shall lay hold upon this our grace and favour, and shall, by any public act, declare their doing so, and that they return to the loyalty and obedience of good subjects; excepting only such persons as shall hereafter be excepted by Parliament ...

The subsequent Indemnity and Oblivion Act of the same year excluded the Regicides. Harrison couldn't possibly hope to escape the ultimate sentence at his trial and thus stood bravely by his beliefs and principles. On 13 October 1660 he was taken from Newgate on a hurdle to Charing Cross and was hanged, drawn and quartered.

Pepy's diary entry that day illustrates the almost casual manner that judicial death was observed, for Pepys, having attended one of the grimmest forms of public execution, immediately continued his social plans for the day.

> 'To my Lord's in the morning, where I met with Captain Cuttance, but my Lord not being up I went out to Charing Cross, to see Major-general Harrison hanged, drawn, and quartered; which was done there, he looking as cheerful as any man could do in that condition. He was presently cut down, and his head and heart shown to the people, at which there was great shouts of joy. It is said, that he said that he was sure to come shortly at the right hand of Christ to judge them that now had judged him; and that his wife do expect his coming again. Thus it was my chance to see the King beheaded at White Hall, and to see the first blood shed in revenge for the blood of the King at Charing Cross. From thence to my Lord's, and took Captain Cuttance and Mr. Sheply to the Sun Tavern, and did give them some oysters. ... Within all the afternoon setting up shelves in my study. At night to bed.'

The magnificently titled '*An Exact and Impartial Accompt Of the Indictment, Arraignment, Tryal, and Judgment (according to Law) of Twenty Nine Regicides, The Murtherers of His Late Sacred Majesty Of Most Glorious Memory* ... published in London in 1679 summarised the fate of a number of the regicides:

> 'Thus having given the Reader a most impartial view of every Passage occurring in this so solemn and legal Indictment, Arraignment, Trial, and Condemnation of these twenty nine black Regicides, with their several Pleas and Defences in their own words. It may be also some additional satisfaction, to let the Reader know the time and manner of such of them who were according to the Sentence Executed. For their last Discourses and Prayers, as they were made in a Croud, and therefore not possible to be taken exactly; so it was thought fit rather to say nothing, than give an untrue account thereof; chusing rather to appear lame, than to be supported with imperfect assistances.'

According to the *State Trials*, Harrison showed no fear.

'The Sheriff came [to Newgate] that morning that he was to die, and told him, that in half an hour he must be gone; he answered that he was ready, and would not have him stay at all on his account. But the sheriff left him to stay a little longer, and in the mean time, he was longing for the sheriff's coming, and all his friends judged he was in haste to be gone, and said, He was going about a great work for the Lord that day; and that his support was, that his sufferings were upon the account of Jehovah, the Lord of Hosts ... He parted with his wife and friends with great joy and chearfulness....'

On arriving at Charing Cross he hugged his servant and 'went up the ladder with an undaunted countenance; from whence he spake to the multitude ...' Just how important one's behaviour at the scaffold was, and how every minutiae was noted, can be seen from an observation of a slight tremble in his hand and one of his legs. On noting that this had been seen, Harrison, during the course of his speech beneath the gallows said, 'Gentlemen, By reason of some scoffing that I do hear, I judge that some do think I am afraid to die, by the shaking I have in my hands and knees; I tell you, no, but it is by reason of much blood I have lost in the wars, and many wounds I have received in my body, which caused this shaking and weakness in my nerves ...'[3] His speech continued at some length and the sheriff had to remind him of the shortness of time. The *State Trials* note that on finishing he was 'turned off, and was cut down, alive, for after his body was opened, he mounted himself, and gave the executioner a box on the ear.'[4] Ludlow commented that the sentence was carried out in a barbaric manner. The Exact and Impartial Accompt Of the Indictment volume fills in some detail:

63. The statue of Charles I, in the southern part of Trafalgar Square, was placed there in 1675 on the site of the executions of the regicides and looking towards the Banqueting House where Charles I was beheaded.

'On Saturday the 13th of October 1660, betwixt nine and ten of the clock in the Morning, Mr. Tho. Harrison, or, Major General Harrison, according to this sentence, was upon a Hurdle drawn from Newgate to the place called Charing-Cross; where within certain Rails lately there made, a Gibbet was erected, and he hanged with his face looking towards the Banqueting-house at Whitehall, (the place where our late Sovereign of eternal memory was sacrificed) being half dead, he was cut down by the common Executioner, his Privy Members cut off before his eyes, his Bowels burned, his Head severed from his Body, and his Body divided into Quarters, which were returned back to Newgate upon the same Hurdle that carried it. His Head is since set on a Pole on the top of the South-East end of Westminster-Hall, looking towards London. The Quarters of his Body are in like manner exposed upon some of the City Gates.

Monday following, being the fifteenth of October, about the same hour, Mr. John Carew was carried in the like manner to the same place of Execution; where having suffered like pains, his Quarters were also returned to Newgate on the same Hurdle which carried him.'

Of Carew, the *State Trials* tell us that he was cheerful all the way to the gibbet, 'setting forth his joy in the Lord.' On the ladder he made a lengthy speech, and again the sheriff interrupted suggesting that he now pray. After the completion of his prayers he bade farewell to his friends telling them that 'we part with much joy in our souls.' He was then executed in the manner of Harrison. Evelyn's diary entry notes that 'Scot, Scroop, Cook, and Jones, suffered for reward of their iniquities at Charing Cross, in sight of the place where they put to death their natural prince, and in the presence of the King, his son, whom they also sought to kill.' He writes, 'I saw not their execution, but met their quarters, mangled and cut, and reeking, as they were brought from the gallows in baskets on the hurdle.'[5]

> 'Tuesday following, being the sixteenth of October, Master John Cook, and Mr. Hugh Peters, were about the same hour carried on two Hurdles to the same place, and executed in the same manner, and their Quarters returned in like manner to the place whence they came. The Head of John Cook is since set on a Pole on the North-East end of Westminster-Hall (on the left of Mr. Harrison's) looking towards London; and the head of Mr. Peters on London-Bridg. Their Quarters are exposed in like manner upon the tops of some of the City Gates.'

John Cook, who was executed on Wednesday, 17 October, made a speech justifying his cause, which led the sheriff to interrupt and admonish him on a number of occasions. He drew to a close making reference to his 'poor wife and child' and hoped that Parliament would not sequester what he left to them.

> 'Wednesday, October 17, about the hour of nine in the morning, Mr. Thomas Scot, and Mr. Gregory Clemen, were brought in several Hurdles; and about one hour after Master Adrian Scroop and Mr. John Jones together in one Hurdle were carried to the same place, and suffered the same death, and were returned and disposed of in the like manner.'

Francis Hacker and Daniel Axtel probably on account of the public backlash against the cruelty being shown at Charing Cross were executed at Tyburn instead:

> 'Mr. Francis Hacker, and Mr. Daniel Axtel, were on Friday the 19th of October, about the same time of the morning, drawn on one Hurdle from Newgate to Tiburn, and there both Hanged; Mr. Axtel was Quartered, and returned back, and disposed as the former; but the Body of Mr. Hacker was, by his Majesties great favour, given entire to his Friends, and buried.

1 *The diary of Henry Machyn ... from AD 1550 to AD 1563*, ed. J G Nichols, Camden Society Publication 42 (1848), p. 73

2 *Ibid*, p. 86

3 *State Trials*, vol. 5 p. 1235

4 *Ibid*. p. 1235

5 John Evelyn. *Diary and Correspondence of John Evelyn F R S*. (London, George Bell and Sons, 1881), pp. 360-361

CHAPTER SEVEN

Old and New Palace Yards Westminster

Old and New Palace Yards were part and parcel of the old Palace of Westminster, now the Houses of Parliament. They still exist, though in a different form, within the present building's complex. Old Palace Yard lies west of the St Stephen's entrance to the House of Lords. New Palace Yard is a small garden on top of the MPs' car park to the north of Westminster Hall. The Hall, originally built in 1097-9 but given its famous hammerbeam roof in 1399, is the oldest part of the Palace. it was the setting for the trials of William Wallace (1305), Sir Thomas More (1535), the Gunpowder Plot conspirators (1606) and Charles I (1649).

At New Palace Yard a Puritan attorney, John Stubs, along with his servant and Robert Page, had their hands cut off for libelling Elizabeth I. Not long afterwards a William Parry was hanged, drawn and quartered for treason. In 1612, Lord Sanquire was hanged here, in front of Westminster Hall for murder.[1]

At Old Palace Yard died some Gunpowder Plot conspirators, while others were despatched at St Paul's Churchyard. Sir Walter Raleigh was executed here after many years of imprisonment in the Tower.

64. *Sir Walter Raleigh. Oil painting by Hubert L. Smith.*

The Execution of Sir Walter Raleigh at Old Palace Yard

Sir Walter Raleigh (*c*.1552-1618) first tasted prison life when Queen Elizabeth discovered that he had secretly married one of her ladies-in-waiting in 1592. He gradually returned to favour but in 1603 he was tried for treason due to his implicated involvement in the Rye House Plot against James I. He was found guilty though spared execution and remained in the Tower of London until 1616, during which time he wrote a number of historical works. He was then freed to search for El Dorado and during this expedition he sanctioned the sacking of a Spanish outpost on the river Orinoco, during which his own son, also Walter, was killed. On Raleigh's return to England an outraged Spanish ambassador demanded that the suspended death sentence on Raleigh be carried out, to which the King agreed. Raleigh was held in the Tower until his execution on 29 October, 1618.

65. The execution of Sir Walter Raleigh.

66. Plaque to Raleigh in St Margaret's church, Westminster. It sits ignominiously in a corner between a cupboard and some fire extinguishers. It reads: 'Within ye chancel of this church was interred the body of the great Sr Walter Raleigh K^{t} on the day he was beheaded in Old Palace Yard, Westminster Oct. 29th an^{o} Dom. 1618. Reader - should you reflect on his errors - remember his many virtues - and that he was a mortal.'

On that day, it was related,

'It was now near nine, and having declared himself ready he was led to the place of execution, in the Old Palace Yard, by the Sheriffs of London and the Dean of Westminster. A great crowd had assembled, and as many pushed forward to gaze on him, among the rest one venerable old man, whose head was quite bald, came so near that Sir Walter noticed him and inquired if he wanted ought with him; the old man answered, that his only desire was to see him, and to pray God for him: "I thank thee, my good friend, " said Raleigh, "and am sorry I am in no case to return thee anything for thy good-will. But," he added, looking at his bald head, "here, take this nightcap," removing that which he wore beneath his hat, "thou hast more need of it now than I."[2]

Shortly, in a very leisured, stately and gentlemanly manner, Raleigh reached the scaffold:

'The people pressed him so much that, faint from sickness, he had nearly swooned away before he reached the scaffold, which was erected in front of the parliament-house ... On coming to the steps he recovered, mounted them easily, and saluted those who stood near with the same graceful courtesy which usually distinguished his manners. Proclamation was then made for silence, and Raleigh standing up, although very feeble, addressed those around him. His last words have been transmitted to us by several persons who were present, and we read them almost exactly as he delivered them ...'

Raleigh was concerned that, not feeling well, his weakness would be taken to be a sign of fear. He made it clear to those around him, it was not fear that caused him to shake:

67. St Mary's church, West Horsley, near Guildford. The chapel holds the head of Raleigh and his son Carew.

'I have had for these two days past, two fits of an ague. Yesterday I was, notwithstanding, taken out of my bed in one of my fits, and whether I shall escape it this day or not I cannot tell. If therefore, you perceive any weakness in me, I beseech you ascribe it to my sickness rather than to myself.'

There then followed a lengthy vindication of his innocence, read from prepared notes. So weak from illness was he that in the middle he was compelled to sit down. His words were spoken 'with grace and animation'. Drawing to a close, he then embraced the many assembled lords who stood with him on the scaffold and asked them to ensure that no defamatory matter would be published after his death.

Comfort on the Scaffold

The morning was cold and the Sheriff suggested to Raleigh that he come down off the scaffold and warm himself in front of a fire before saying his prayers. Raleigh replied, 'No, good Mr Sheriff, let us despatch, for within this quarter of an hour my ague will come upon me, and if I be not dead before that, mine enemies shall say I quake for fear.'[13]

The Execution

After saying prayers Raleigh arose and said that he was now 'going to God!' The scaffold was cleared of unnecessary personnel in preparation. Raleigh took off his gown and doublet and then asked the executioner to show him the axe. There was a pause as there was an initial reluctance to do this - possibly in case it would cause him to show fear, and it was usual for this reason that the axe was hidden. Raleigh repeated his request. 'I prithee let me see it. Dost thou think I am afraid of it?' Running his fingers along the edge of the blade he commented to the Sheriff that the axe 'tis a sharp medicine, but a sound cure for all diseases.'

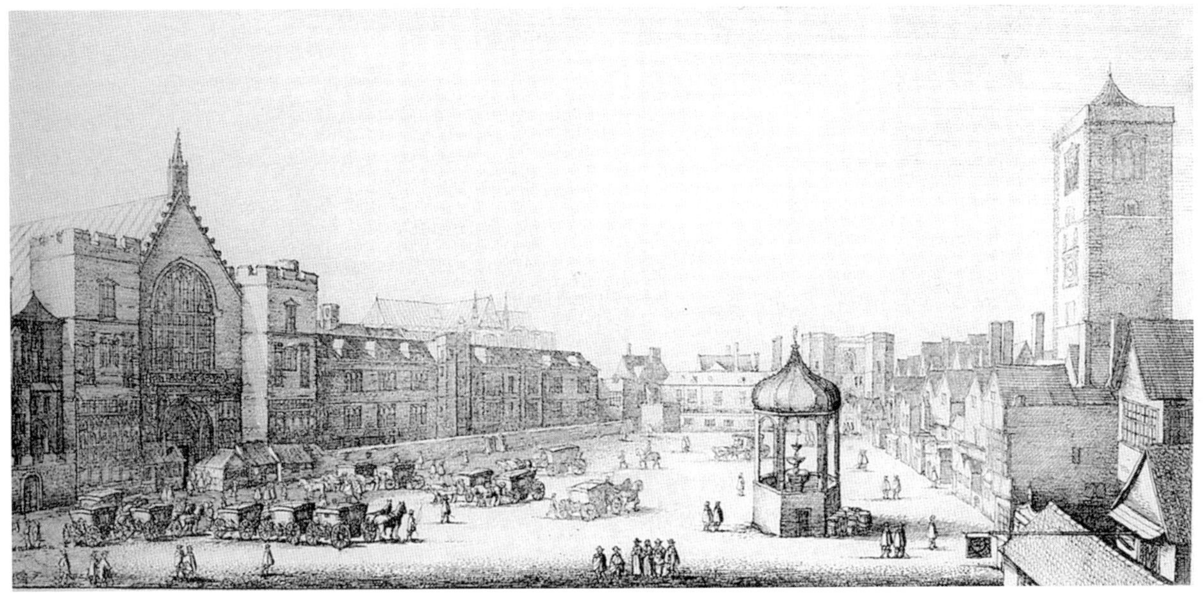

68. *New Palace Yard, drawn by Wenceslaus Hollar in 1647. The north front of Westminster Hall is to the left and a clock tower, the forerunner of Big Ben, is to the right.*

69. *New Palace Yard today, over the MPs' car park.*

70. *Old Palace Yard in the 18th century.*

71. *The area of Old Palace Yard today, by the entrance to St Stephen's Tower.*

Kneeling down he prayed and requested those around him to pray for him. He then stood up again and examined the block 'laying himself down to fit it to his neck and to choose the easiest and most decent attitude ...' He stood up yet again declaring himself ready, at which point the executioner came forward and asked, as was customary, Raleigh's forgiveness. He then said that when he gave the signal the executioner should 'fear nothing and strike home.' He then again lay down and put his head on the block at which point the executioner asked if he could 'face to the east ...' Raleigh prayed further and gave the signal for the executioner to strike, but for some reason the executioner hesitated. Raleigh then partially raised his head saying 'what dost thou fear? Strike, man!'

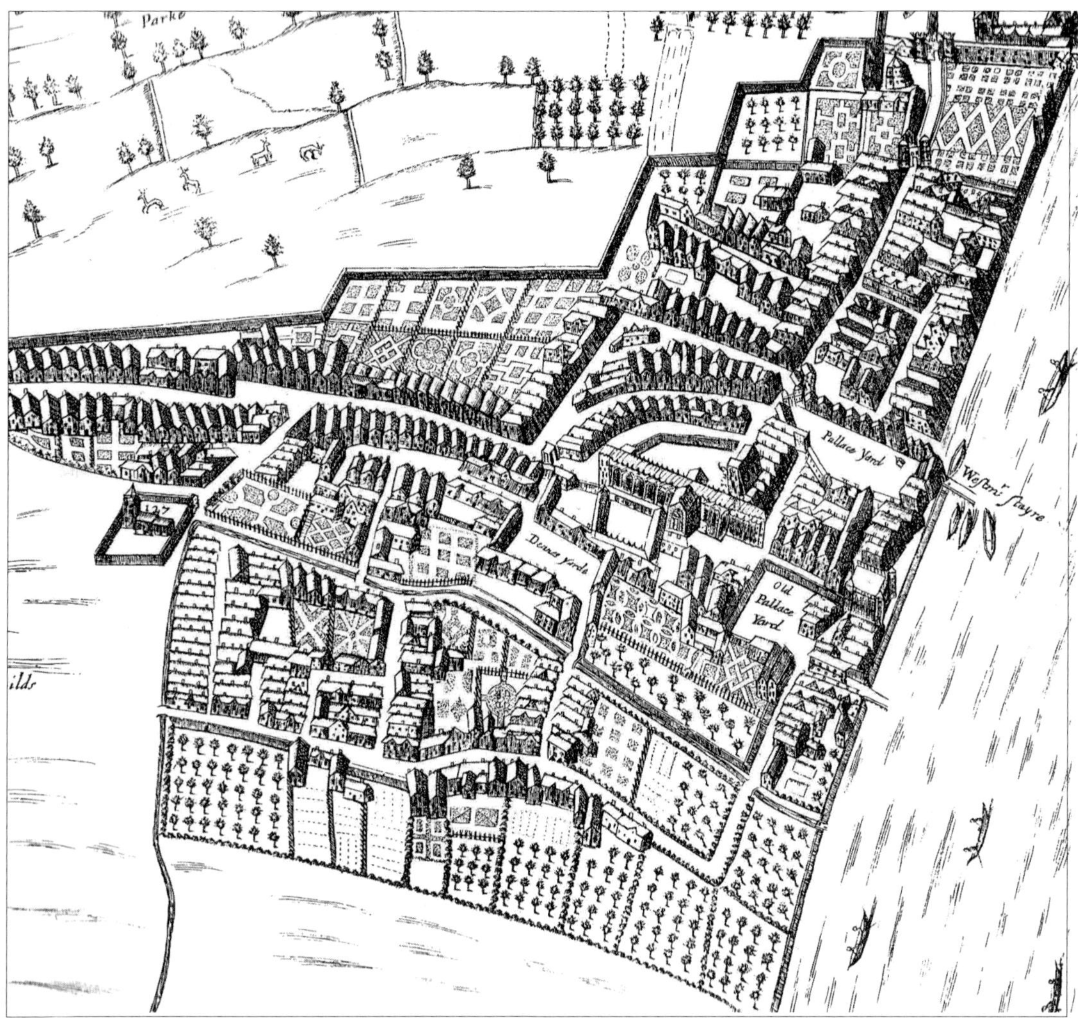

72. *The Palace of Westminster in 1658.*

Raleigh's Head

After being displayed to the crowd, Raleigh's head was placed in a red bag, over which his velvet nightgown was thrown and the whole being carried to a mourning coach waiting nearby. The remains were conveyed to Lady Raleigh who had the head embalmed and preserved in a case. The remainder of his body was buried in an unmarked grave near the altar of St Margaret's church, Westminster.

His wife survived him by 29 years. After her death, his son Carew kept the head, and on his own death it was buried with him in St Margaret's. The body of Carew and his father's head, were later exhumed and reinterred in St Mary's church, West Horsley, Surrey, near the family seat, which was not far from Guildford. Raleigh's body still lies in St Margaret's where there is a memorial plaque.[4]

The church of St Mary in West Horsley dates from 1030. It contains well preserved 13th-century wall paintings. Raleigh's head and the remains of his son Carew lie unmarked beneath the floor of the chapel, behind the organ. A letter written by William Nicholas, who owned Raleigh's former estate in the 18th century and whose remains also reside in the chapel, records that 'the head he saw dug up there in 1703, from the side of a grave where a Carew Raleigh had been buried, was that of Sir Walter Raleigh, there being no bones of a body to it, nor room for any, the rest of that side of the grave being firm chalk.'

The Gunpowder Plot

The plot to blow up the Houses of Parliament and reinstate Roman Catholicism as the country's religion was aborted on 5 November 1605 when one of the conspirators, Guy Fawkes, charged with the actual deed, was discovered in the cellars of Parliament together with 36 barrels of gunpowder. These, seemingly, had been transported piecemeal across the river from a house in Lambeth.

The leader of the conspirators, Robert Catesby, was fortunate in being killed resisting arrest in the Midlands and did not stand trial or endure the certain punishment at the gallows, but eight other conspirators suffered excessive interrogation before being tried and sentenced to the sort of execution reserved for those who committed treason. Guy Fawkes, for example, had been tortured to such an extent that the signature on his confession is barely readable, and he had to be helped up the steps of the ladder at his execution. The four to die in Old Palace Yard were Thomas Winter, Ambrose Rookwood, Robert Keyes and Fawkes.

State Trials deals briefly with the fate of the Westminster victims:

> 'The next day, being Friday, were drawn from the Tower, to the Old Palace in Westminster, Thomas Winter, Rookwood, Keyes and Fawkes, where Winter, first being brought to the scaffold, made little speech, but seeming after a sort, as it were, sorry for his offence, and yet crossing himself, as though these were words ... went up to the Ladder, and after a swing or two with a halter, to the quartering block was drawn, and there quickly despatched.'[5]

It is clear that only two swings on the gallows was a deliberate act so that disembowelling and quartering could be carried out whilst Winter was alive and conscious. The next to be executed was Rookwood,

> '... who made a speech of some longer time, confessing his offence to God, in seeking to shed blood ... But last of all, to mar all the pottage with

73. The execution of Guy Fawkes in 1606.

> one filthy weed ... he prayed God to make the king a catholick, otherwise a papist ... protesting to die in his idolatry, a Romish Catholick, he went up the ladder, and, hanging till he was almost dead, was drawn to the block, where he gave his last gasp.'

Keyes, who followed, showed no repentance and 'went stoutly up the ladder' off which he jumped attempting to break his own neck, but the halter broke, and he fell to the ground. Rather than hang him again, the executioner took him straight to the block where he was quartered. The *State Trials* tell us that

> 'Last of all came the great devil of Fawkes ... who should have put fire to the powder. His body was weak with torture and sickness, and he was scarcely able to go up the ladder, but yet with ado, by the help of the hangman, went high enough to break his neck with the fall: who made no long speech, but, after a sort, seeming to be sorry for his offence, asked a kind of forgiveness of the king and the state for his blood intent; and, with his crosses and his idle ceremonies, made his end upon the gallows and the block, to the great joy of the beholders, that the land was ended of so wicked a villainy.'

Civil War Executions, 9 March 1649

After the execution of Charles I in 1649, a number of his commanders and supporters were captured, tried at Westminster Hall, and sentenced to die all on the same day, Friday, 9 March, 1649.

At ten in the morning the Duke of Hamilton (bn 1606), the Earl of Holland (bn *c.*1590) and Arthur, Lord Capel (bn 1604) were summoned from St James's Palace under armed sedan to the home of Sir Thomas Cotton in Westminster where they were allowed to remain for prayers and conversation for about two hours before being summoned to the scaffold. The executions took place on a scaffold in New Palace Yard, 'over against the great hall gate, in the site of the place where the high court of justice formerly sat, the hall doors being open...'[16]

Hamilton said goodbye to his friends and prepared to go first to the scaffold attended by his servants. There were lengthy prayers until he was ready.

Duke: 'I shall say a very short prayer to my God, while I lay down there; and when I stretch out my hand, my right hand, then, sir, do your duty; and I do freely forgive you, and so I do all the world.'

He then again made some religious utterances before turning again to the executioner:

Duke: Must I lie along?

Executioner: Yes, and't please your lordship.

Duke: When I stretch out my hands ... But I will fit my head first; tell me if I be right, and how you would have me lie.

Executioner: Your shirt must be pinn'd back, for it lies too high upon your shoulders. (This was then done.)

Dr Sibbald (Chaplain) My lord, now lift up your eyes to Jesus Christ, and cast yourself now into the everlasting arms of your gracious Redeemer.

The Duke then lay on the block and for a short while prayed, then stretched out his right hand and the executioner removed his head with one blow of the axe. Hamilton's servants immediately wrapped the head in a crimson scarf, and placed it in the coffin that waited on the scaffold, along with the body. It was then taken to Sir John Hamilton's house 'at the mews'.

The Sheriff's guard then immediately sent for the Earl of Holland.

The Earl of Holland

Henry Rich, 1st Earl of Holland was incensed that he was brought to the block. He had been promised a pardon when he had surrendered to the Parliamentarians, but was tried and sentenced to death, and on his petition to Parliament only the casting vote of the Speaker of the House of Commons had told against him. However, he was so ill by the time he came to the scaffold that it was believed he would have died in a few days anyway.

The account of his execution suggests a man uneasy with the protocols of the scaffold:

Holland: (to the executioner): Here, my friend,

74. Henry Rich, 1st Earl of Holland; oil from the studio of Daniel Mytens.

let my cloaths and my body alone; there is ten pounds for thee, that is better than my cloaths, I am sure of it.

Executioner: Will your lordship please to give me a sign when I shall strike?

Holland: You have room enough here, have you not?

Executioner: Yes

Holland: Friend, do you hear me? If you take up my head, do not take off my cap ... Stay, I will kneel down, and ask God forgiveness.

Holland: Which is the way of lying? (He is shown, and then walks to the front of the scaffold to address the crowd.) He blesses them and wishes them happiness. He then turns to the executioner:

Holland: How must I lie? I know not.

Executioner: Lie down flat upon your belly.

Holland then lay down and spoke to the executioner.

Holland: Must I lie closer?

Executioner: Yes, and backwarder.

Holland: I will tell you when you shall strike.

Holland then stretched out his hand catching the executioner by surprise. He had to shout Now! Now! twice before the axe struck.[7]

Arthur, Lord Capel

Dr Morley, Bishop of Winchester, wrote to Edward Symonds, Capel's chaplain informing him that he was

> 'there at the time assigned ... But he was to have an agony before his passion; and that was the parting with his wife, eldest son, son-in-law, two of his uncles, and Sir Thomas Corbet, especially the parting with his most dear lady; which was the saddest spectacle that I ever beheld ... in blessing the young lord, he commanded him never to revenge his death, though it should be in his power. The like he said unto his Lady ... After this, with much adoe I persuaded his wife and the rest to be gone: and then being all alone with me, he said, 'Doctor, the hardest part of my work in this world, is now past'.

The bishop went with Capel to Sir Robert Cotton's house. He says in the letter that he was not allowed to go on the scaffold with him. On being escorted to the scaffold Capel doffed his cap to people on both sides of the crowd. On mounting the scaffold he was 'greeted' by the parliamentary minder, Lieutenant-Colonel Beecher, who asked him if he had come with his chaplain, to which Capel replied he had not as he had already taken leave of him. Capel was surrounded by weeping servants and asked Beecher if he should make his speech with his hat off, the answer to which was in the affirmative. At the end of a short speech he turned around looking for the executioner who was not at this time on the scaffold and asked 'which is the gentleman, which is the man?' To which he was answered 'he is coming.'

Capel: Stay, I must pull off my doublet first and my waistcoat.

The executioner stepped onto the scaffold.

Capel: Oh my friend! Pr'ythee come hither.

The executioner knelt down and asked Capel's forgiveness.

Capel: I forgive thee, but I shall pray God to give thee all grace for a better life. There is five pounds for thee, and truly, for my clothes, and those things, if there be any due to you for it, you shall be full recompensed: but I desire my body may not be stripped here, and no body to take notice of my body but my own servants. Look you, friend, this I shall desire of you, that when I lie down, you would give me a time for a particular short prayer.

Lieut. Col. Beecher: Make your own sign my lord.

Capel: Stay a little. Which side do you stand upon? Stay I think I should lay my hands forward that way (pointing forward to the right).

Capel then turned to his servant, Baldwin:

Capel: Baldwin I cannot see anything that belongs to my wife; but I desire thee, and beseech her, to rest wholly upon Jesus Crhist, to be contented and fully satisfied. Capel then turned to his servants.

Capel: Pray at the moment of striking join your prayers, but make no noise ... it is inconvenient at this time.

Servant: My lord put on your cap.

Capel: Should I, what will that do me good? (he put up his hair) Stay a little, it is as well as it is now. Then turning to the executioner,

Capel: Honest man, I have forgiven thee, therefore strike boldly; from my soul I do it ... Well you are ready when I am ready, are you not ...

He then walked to the front of the scaffold and speaking to the crowd:

Capel: Gentlemen, tho' I doubt not of it, yet I think it convenient to ask of you, that you would all join in prayers with me, that God would mercifully receive my soul, and that for his alone mercies in Christ Jesus. God Almighty keep you all.

Executioner: My lord shall I put up your hair?

Capel: I, prythee do (lifting up his hands and eyes) O God, I do, with a perfect and willing heart, submit to thy will. O God, I do most willingly humble myself. (Kneeling down) I will try first how I can lye. (He lay his head on the block and addressed the executioner)

Capel: Am I well now?

Executioner: yes

Capel: Here lie both my hands out, when I lift up my hand thus .... (he lifted his right hand) you may strike.

He then made a short prayer, lifted his right hand, the executioner struck severing Capel's head with one blow. His servants placed his body in the waiting coffin, and it was transferred to the family seat, Hadham Hall in Essex.[8] His body was then placed in the family vault in Little Hadham church, and an outpsoken inscription placed on the tomb stone which may still be seen:

Here under lyeth interred the body of Arthur Capell Baron of Hadham who was murdered for his Loyalty to King Charles the First March 9th 1648 [1649].

Here lyeth ye body of Elizabeth Lady Capell Wife of Arthur Lord Capell

Onely daughter of Sr Charles Morrison Kt She departed this life ye 26th of Jan, 1660.

1 Edward Walford, *Old and New London*, vol. 3 (1878), pp 536-44

2 P. F. Tytler, *Life of Sir Walter Raleigh*, (Edinburgh, 1833), pp 371-372

3 *Ibid*, pp 363-366

4 Sir Walter Raleigh, *The Works of Sir Walter Ralegh Kt*, commentary by Thomas Birch (1827)

I am grateful for the assistance of Patricia Davis of St Mary's Church Office, West Horsley for dealing with my queries so helpfully.

5 *State Trials*, 1606, pp 216-217

6 Source used and adapted is D. Gordon, *A general history of the lives, trials, and executions of all the royal and noble personages that have suffered in Great-Britain and Ireland for high treason, or other crimes....* (1760), pp 476-488

7 *Ibid*, pp 502-503

8 *Ibid*, pp 504-510

CHAPTER EIGHT

Tower Green

The location of the scaffold at Tower Green is not known exactly. Furthermore only seven people are known to have been executed here. The victims were buried a short distance away in St. Peter ad Vincula, which lies directly behind the area of execution. The scaffold was built specially for each execution, and not always put precisely in the same place. Those executed here were William, Lord Hastings (June 1483); Anne Boleyn (19 May 1536); Margaret Pole, Countess of Salisbury (27 May, 1541); Catherine Howard (13 February, 1542), and executed on the same day Jane, Viscountess Rochford; Lady Jane Grey (12 February, 1554); and Robert Devereux, Earl of Essex (25 February 1601). The area, inside the walls of the Tower, was enclosed and protected against unruly crowds.

75. Anne Boleyn.

Anne Boleyn

Anne Boleyn (*c.* 1500-19 May 1536) was the daughter of the Earl of Wiltshire and the second wife of Henry VIII. The events leading to the scaffold are well known and the charges against her included adultery, incest and treason. It is possible through eyewitness accounts to reconstruct the events of her final day. Kingston, the Constable of the Tower wrote to Thomas Cromwell, Henry's faithful servant:

> 'This morning she sent for me, that I might be with her at such time as she received the good Lord, to the intent I should hear her speak as touching her innocency always to be clear. And in the writing of this she sent for me, and at my coming she said, "Mr. Kingston, I hear I shall not die afore noon, and I am very sorry therefore, for I thought to be dead by this time and past my pain." I told her it should be no pain, it was so little. And then she said, "I heard say the executioner was very good, and I have a little neck" and then put her hands about it, laughing heartily. I have seen many men and also women executed, and that they have been in great sorrow, and to my knowledge this lady has much joy in death. Sir, her almoner is continually with her, and had been since two o'clock after midnight.'[1]

Her nerve held even onto the scaffold:

'All these being on a scaffold made there for the execution, the said Queen Anne said as followeth: "Masters, I here humbly submit me to the law, as the law hath judged me, and as for mine offences,

76. St Peter ad Vincula at the Tower of London, mid 18th century. The bricked-up windows have subsequently been uncovered.

God knoweth them, I remit them to God, beseeching him to have mercy on my soul; and I beseech Jesu save my Sovereign and master the King, the most goodliest, and gentlest Prince that is, and long to reign over you", which words she spake with a smiling countenance: which done, she kneeled down on both her knees, and said, "To Jesu Christ I commend my soul" and with that word suddenly the hangman of Calais smote off her head at one stroke with a sword: her body with the head was buried in the choir of the Chapel in the Tower.'[2]

Tytler gives us the following account:

'...and, on the 19th of May Anne was led from her chamber in the Tower to the scaffold, which had been prepared for her on the green within that fortress. It was surrounded by those only whom the jealous precautions of Henry had selected to be witnesses rather than spectators; the Dukes of Suffolk and Richmond, the Lord Chancellor Audley, Secretary Cromwell, and the Mayor and Aldermen of London. She ascended the platform with a countenance in which composure and sweetness were strongly depicted, and casting her eyes upon those who stood around it, spoke these few words: "Good Christian people, I am come hither to die according to law; by the law I am judged to die, and therefore I will speak nothing against it, — I am hither to accuse no man, nor to speak anything of that whereof I am accused. I pray God save the king, and send him long to reign over you; for a gentler or more merciful prince was there never. To me he was ever a good, gentle, and sovereign lord, and if any person will meddle with my cause, I require them to judge the best; and thus I take my leave of the world and of you all, and I heartily desire you all to pray for me." Having said this, she removed the hat and collar, which might have impeded the stroke, and meekly kneeling down, exclaimed in an audible voice, "Christ, I pray thee, receive my soul." Whilst she was yet repeating these words, the sword descended , and at one blow her head was severed from her body." Such was the miserable fate of this beautiful and once highly-favoured queen.....'

The speech itself sounds too contrived and forgiving of Henry to be genuine. Anne Boleyn neither confesses nor denies her guilt, and there is absolutely no condemnation of the man that had sent her to the scaffold. But it is easy to forget in the controlled manner of the speech that she was a matter of minutes from her death and looking to preserve her daughter, the future Elizabeth I, from any act of Henry's well-known vindictiveness.

Margaret Pole

Margaret Pole, Countess of Salisbury (*c*.1473-1541) was the daughter of George Plantagenet and Isabella Neville. Her father being a brother to two kings, Edward IV and Richard III, she was the last survivor of the Plantagenet dynasty. In the tumultous times of that period Henry VIII doubtless felt that it would be too dangerous to allow her to live. At a time of religious strife and conflict with Rome, loyalty to the Catholic church could be seen as an act of treason. She was arrested at the behest of Thomas Cromwell who introduced a Bill of Attainder against her in the May of 1539. She was immediately sent to the Tower where for two years she was kept under harsh conditions. In April 1541 there was an uprising in the north of England, and Henry, in his usual ruthless manner, believed it would be safer to remove a possible focus of discontent. On the morning of May 27, she was told that she had an hour to prepare for her death. Her response was that she had not committed any crime. She was then taken to Tower Green where a low wooden block had been placed. There were 150 witnesses to the events that followed, and accounts of what happened vary. One, which originated with the main chronicler of the life of Henry VIII, Lord Herbert of Cherbury, is likely to be the most accurate:

77. Margaret Pole, Countess of Salisbury. Oil by an unknown artist c. 1535.

'... She was the last lineal descendent of the Plantagenets; and, although past seventy years of age, possessed a masculine courage and spirit which was worthy of that race. On being designed to lay her neck on the block, she refused, declaring that it belonged to traitors to do so, and bidding the executioner take her life as he best could. Thus dared in the performance of his office, a horrid scene occurred; the countess moved swiftly round the scaffold, tossing her head from one side to the other, and avoiding the blows which were aimed at her; nor was the appalling spectacle concluded till her grey locks which streamed over her shoulders were covered with blood.'[3]

Catherine Howard

Catherine Howard was born *c.* 1520, the daughter of Lord Edmund Howard and Joyce Culpepper, and the niece of the Duke of Norfolk. She was also the first cousin of Anne Boleyn, Henry's second wife. She was poorly educated, and it is

78. Catherine Howard, after Hans Holbein the Younger.

believed that her upbringing in the licentious atmosphere of the Duchess of Norfolk's circle led to a number of relationships. One of these was a romance with Henry Mannox her music teacher, sometime around 1536, when Catherine was aged somewhere between the ages of 12 and 16. After marrying Henry, Catherine unwisely brought Mannox into her household. It is not known whether they resumed their relationship - both denied it when the matter was brought up at her trial, though she admitted to some physical contact with him. In 1538 Catherine had fallen for Francis Dereham, a young secretary. At the insistence of the Dowager Duchess of Norfolk this relationship was terminated in 1539, but both parties promised to marry at some later date. Her uncle, the Duke of Norfolk, found Catherine a position at court as a lady-in-waiting to Henry's then Queen, Anne of Cleves. Henry quickly found himself attracted to the vivacious Catherine, whose standing was increasingly promoted by the Howard family as a means of gaining political influence. Henry's marriage to Anne was annulled and Henry very soon showered Catherine with gifts, and it was rumoured that she was pregnant by him. Henry married her quickly, probably in the hope of fathering a son.

Henry was nearly 50, and Catherine was around 30 years younger. It transpired that she was not pregnant, and found Henry physically repugnant. Foolishly, in the open and gossip-ridden atmosphere of the court, she embarked on a romance with one of Henry's courtiers, Thomas Culpepper. This was encouraged and facilitated by one of Catherine's ladies-in-waiting, Lady Rochford. Catherine's activities, both before and after her marriage to Henry, particularly with Francis Dereham, were too well known to be kept secret and in the end, by late 1541, these rumours reached Thomas Cranmer, Archbishop of Canterbury, and an advisor to Henry.

Henry refused at first to believe the accusations against Catherine, but after being tortured in the Tower, both Dereham and Culpepper had confessed. She was arrested on 12 November 1541. Initially she was allowed to remain at Syon House, whilst the legalities of charging the Queen went on in the background. Once these had been finalised she was taken amidst a hysterical frenzy to the Tower during the course of which she had to be forced into a barge on the Thames, by the Duke of Suffolk. This was on Friday, 10 February 1542. She was lodged in the Queen's Apartments, which still remain overlooking Tower Green.

Contemporary accounts of the demise of Catherine Howard are scarce, the best known being that of the Spanish ambassador of the time, Eustace Chapuys.

> 'This year on 13 November Sir Thomas Wriothesley, secretary to the king, came to Hampton Court to the queen, and called all the ladies and gentlewomen and her servants into the great chamber, and there openly before them declared certain offenses she had committed in misusing her body with certain persons before the king's time, because of which he there discharged all her household; and the morning after she was taken to Sion, with my Lady Bainton

and two other gentlewomen and certain of her servants to wait on her there until the king's further pleasure. And various people were taken to the Tower of London, such as my Lady Rochford, Master Culpepper, one of the king's privy chamber, and others.

On 1 December Thomas Culpepper, one of the gentlemen of the king's privy chamber, and Francis Dorand [Dereham], gentleman, were arraigned at the Guildhall in London, for high treason against the king's majesty, in misdemeanor with the queen, as appeared by their indictment which they confessed to, and they were sentenced to be drawn, hanged, and quartered, the lord mayor sitting there as chief, the lord chancellor on his right hand, and the duke of Norfolk on his left hand, the duke of Suffolk, the lord privy seal, the earls of Sussex, of Hertford, and various others of the king's council sitting with all the judges also in commission that day. And on 10 December the said Culpepper and Dorand were drawn from the Tower of London to Tyburn, and there Culpepper, after exhorting the people to pray for him, stood on the ground by the gallows, knelt down and had his head struck off; and then Dorand was hanged, dismembered, disembowelled, beheaded and quartered. Culpepper's body was buried at St Sepulchre's church near Newgate, and their heads were set on London Bridge.'

As for Catherine, her demise came quickly when on the evening of Sunday, 12 February evening she was informed that she would die at 7am the next day, the 13th. She requested the block be brought to her so that she could rehearse the final act of placing her head on the block. Despite her fear she managed to undertake the ritual of the scaffold, giving a short, quiet speech in which she acknowledged the legitimacy of her punishment and prayed for Henry's preservation, and God's forgiveness. She was interred in the chapel of St. Peter ad Vincula.

Lady Jane Grey

One of the earliest sources for the demise of Lady Jane Grey is a pocket diary[4] covering the period from July 1553 to October 1554. In a foreword to the printed edition, dated 1850,[5] we are told that 'it is written, or rather scribbled, in so bad a hand' and that 'it is the authority for the interesting account given by Stowe and Holinshed, of the execution of Lord Guilford Dudley and Lady Jane Grey, as well as for the greater part of their narrative of the progress of events whilst the council administered the government of the realm in the name of "Jane the Queene"'. In the Harleian Catalogue it is stated, that 'This book formerly belonged to Mr. John Stowe, who took from thence many passages which may be found in his Annals, at the reign of Queen Mary...'

Jane, born in 1537, was the daughter of Frances Brandon and Henry Grey, Duke of Suffolk. She was also the great -granddaughter of Henry VII and this was a basis of her claim to the throne over Mary, daughter of Henry VIII's first wife. Jane was also married to Guilford Dudley, son of the Duke of Northumberland, the mentor of the young Edward VI. Both families were intent on retaining a Protestant monarch and therefore when Edward neared the end of his short life, they conspired to place Jane on the throne instead of the Catholic Mary. Their plan did not enjoy popular support and, eventually, Suffolk, Jane and Dudley were all executed for treason.

The pocket diary account relates:

'Guilforde Dudley, sone to the late duke of Northumberland, husbande to the lady Jane Grey, daughter of the duke of Suffolke, who at his going out took by the hands Sir Anthony Browne, maister John Throgmorton, and many other gentyllmen, praying them to praie for him; and without the bullwarke [Sir Thomas] Offeley the sheryve received him and brought him to the scaffold, where, after a small declaration, having no gostlye father [a priest] with him, he kneeled downe and said his praiers; then holding up his eyes and hands to God many tymes; and at last, after he had desired the people to pray for him,

79. Lady Jane Grey.

he laide himself along, and his hedd upon the block, which was at one stroke of the axe taken from him.'[6]

The account continues:

Note, the lorde marques [Marquess of Northampton] stode upon the Devyl's towre, and saw the execution. His [Guildford's] carcase thrown into a carre, and his hed in a cloth, he was brought into the chapell within the Tower, wher the lady Jane, whose lodging was in Partrige's house, dyd see his ded carcase taken out of the cart, aswell as she dyd see him before on live on going to his deathe - a sight to hir no lesse than death.

By this tyme was ther a scaffolde made upon the grene over agaynst the White tower, for the saide lady Jane to die apon.... Who with hir husband was appynted to have ben put to deathe the fryday before, but was staied tyll then, for what cause is not knowen, unless yt were because hir father was not then come into the Tower. The saide lady, being nothing abashed neither with feare of her owne deathe, which then approached, neither with the sight of the ded carcasse of hir husbande, when he was brought in to the chappell, cause fourthe, the levetenannt leding hir, in the same gown wherin she was arrayned, hir countenance nothing abashed, neither her eyes anything moysted with teares, although her ij. gentylwomen, mistress Elizabeth Tylney and mistress Eleyn, wonderfully wept, with a boke in her hande, wheron she praied all the way till she came to the saide scaffold wheron when she was mounted, &c.....

The manuscript unfortunately breaks off mid-sentence. The 1850 editor then comments that the diary narrative so far is that which is adopted by both Stow and Holinshed, but at this point Holinshed perhaps embellishes the account with the addition of the words:

'Wereon when she mounted, this noble young ladie, as she was indued with singular gifts both of learning and knowledge, so was she as patient and milde as any lambe at hir execution, and a little before her death uttered these words....'[7]

Such embellishments act as a warning against trusting early verbatim accounts of events. The manuscript then continues with a sub-heading which reads.

The Ende of the lady Jane Dudley, [Grey] daughter of the duke of Suffolk, upon the scaffold, at the houre of her death.

'First, when she mounted upon the scaffold, she sayd to the people standing thereabout: "Good people, I am come hether to die, and by a lawe I am condemned to the same. The facte, in dede, against the quenes highnesse was unlawfull, and the consenting thereunto by me: but touching the procurement and desyre therof by me or on my halfe, I doo wash my handes therof in innocencie, before God, and the face of you, good Christian people, this day," and therewith she wrong her handes, in which she had hir booke. Then she sayd, "I pray you all, good Christan people, to beare me witnesse that I dye a true Christian woman, and that I looke to be saved by none other meane, but only by the mercy of God in the merites of the blood of his only sonne Jesus Christ: and I confesse, when I dyd know the word of God I neglected the same, loved my selfe and the world, and therefore this plague or punyshment is happily and worthily happened unto me for my sins; and yet I thank God of his goodnesse that he hath thus geven me a tyme and respet to repent. And now, good people, while I am alive, I pray you to assist me with your prayers." And then knelyng down, she turned to Feckenham, [the dean of St Paul's] saying, "Shall I say this psalme?" And he said, "Yea." Then she said the psalme of *Miserere mei Deus*, in English, in most devout manner, to the end. Then she stode up and gave her maiden mistris Tilney her gloves and handkercher, and her book to maister Bruges, the lyvetenantes brother; forthwith she untyed her gown. The hangman went to her to help her therewith; then she desyred him to let her alone, and turning towards her two gentlewomen, who helped her off therwith, and also with her frose past and neckercher, geving to her a fayre handkercher to knytte about her eyes. Then the hangman kneeled downe, and asked her forgevenesse, whome she forgave most willingly. Then he willed her to stand upon the strawe: which doing, she sawe the block. Then she sayd, "I pray you dispatch me quickly." Then she kneeled down, saying, "Wil you take it of before I lay me downe?" and the hangman answered her, "No, madame." She tyed the kercher about her eys; then feeling for the blocke, saide, "What shall I do? Where is it?'" One of the standers-by guyding her therunto, she layde her heade down upon the block, and stretched forth her body and said: "Lord, into thy hands I commende my spirite!" And so she ended.'[8]

80. Robert Devereux, Earl of Essex. Oil painting by unknown artist.

Robert Devereux, Earl of Essex

Devereux (1567-1601) was a favourite of Elizabeth I, but fell into disfavour over his mishandling of affairs in Ireland and was further disgraced when he led a a small insurrection in London intended to confront the queen. On 19 February 1601 Essex was tried and found guilty of treason. It is possible that on being condemned he believed the queen would pardon him, for at the height of their passion Elizabeth had given him a ring with the promise that whatever he should commit, if he were to send her the ring she would forgive him. After being condemned it is believed that he gave the ring to his relative Admiral Howard's wife, but her husband, a bitter enemy of Essex, on hearing that she had the ring, forbade that it be passed to the queen. It is said that Elizabeth believed that Essex had chosen to die out of haughtiness and pride rather than plead for mercy but even so, when it came

81. *The execution of Essex, as depicted in* Hallowed Spots of Ancient London *(1862).*

to signing the death warrant she vacillated. A while later, after the execution, when the Admiral's wife was dying, she called Elizabeth to her bed side and confessed that her husband had held the ring back. Elizabeth was overcome with grief and died soon after.

Essex was extremely popular and it was felt that it would be too dangerous to execute him on Tower Hill, and so Tower Green was chosen. He was therefore held in the Tower after his arrest so that he could be executed and interred with the minimum of public attention. He was escorted to the scaffold by the lieutenant of the Tower and sixteen guards at 8am on 25 February 1601. A small seating area was built close to the scaffold for a number of lords to observe the proceedings. Essex was dressed in 'a gowne of wrought velvet, a blacke satin suite, a felt hat blacke, a little ruffe about his necke'.[9] With him were also three clergymen. He gave a short speech or confession and then removed his doublet to reveal a scarlet waistcoat. He then 'lying flat along on the bordes, and laying downe his head and fitting it upon the blocke, his head was severed from his bodie by the axe at three stroaks, but the first deadly and absolutely depryving all sence and motion.' Such was his popularity, that the executioner required the protection of the Sheriff of London to protect him 'from such as would have murthered him.'[10] Essex was buried under the supervision of the Earl of Arundel and Duke of Norfolk in St. Peter ad Vincula.

[1] From a letter from Sir W. Kingston, Constable of the Tower, to Thomas Cromwell, May 19th, 1536.

[2] *Ibid*

[3] P. F. Tytler, *Life of King Henry the Eighth,* (Edinburgh, 1837).

[4] *Harleian MS.*194, British Library

[5] J. G. Nichols, *et al., The Chronicle of Queen Jane, and of two years of Queen Mary, and especially of the rebellion of Sir Thomas Wyat. Written by a Resident in the Tower of London* (pub. 1850).

[6] *Ibid,* p. 68

[7] *Ibid,* p. 69

[8] *Ibid,* pp. 58-59

[9] E. Meteyard, *The hallowed spots of ancient London : historical, biographical and antiquarian sketches, illustrative of places and events made memorable by the struggles of our forefathers for civil and religious freedom.* (1862), p. 61.

[10] *Ibid,* pp. 61-62

CHAPTER NINE

Tower Hill

Location of the Scaffold

Executions of those not noble enough or deserving of privacy took place outside of the Tower enclosure, slightly to the north-west on Tower Hill. The author of *Old and New London* (1878), in attempting to discover the exact place decided that it altered over the centuries but was a locality in its own right.

> 'Hatton, in 1708 mentions Tower Hill as "a spacious place extending round the west and north parts of the Tower, where there are many good new buildings, mostly inhabited by gentry and merchants." The tide of fashion and wealth had not yet set in strongly westward. An old plan of the Tower in 1563 shows us the posts of the scaffold for state criminals, a good deal north of Tower Street and a little northward of Legge Mount, the great north-west corner of the Tower fortifications. In the reign of Edward IV the scaffold was erected at the charge of the king's officers, and many controversies arose at various times, about the respective boundaries, between the City and the Lieutenant of the Tower.'[1]

An execution at Tower Hill in 1780 after the Gordon Riots, suggests that the location could vary:

> 'In 1672 a dreadful fire destroyed one hundred houses in the precincts, and another fire during a great storm in 1734 destroyed thirty buildings. During the Gordon riots of 1780 a Protestant mob, headed by Macdonald, a lame soldier, and two women—one a white and one a negro—armed with swords, were about to demolish the church, as being built in Popish times, when the gentlemen of the London Association arrived, and prevented the demolition. Macdonald and the two women were afterwards hanged for this at a temporary gallows on Tower Hill.[2]

The illustration of the 'Beheading of the Rebel Lords' *(see front jacket illustration)* provides a panoramic illustration of where the scaffold was erected for executions, placing it approximately 500 yards to the north-west of the Bloody Tower, consistent with the illustrations on the earlier London maps.

Sir Thomas Wyatt

The accession to the throne of Mary I was perceived as threatening the Protestant

82. Sir Thomas Wyatt.

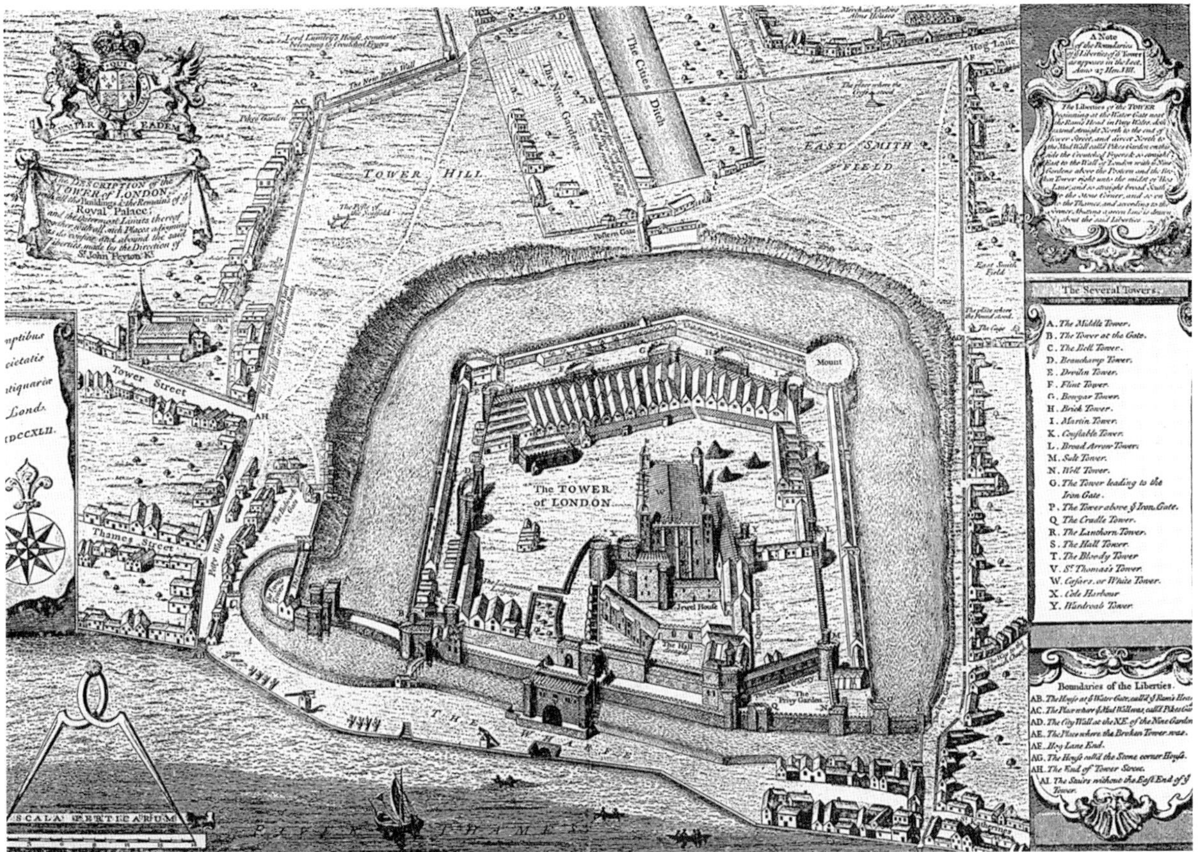

83. A perspective view of the Tower of London, surveyed in 1597 by William Haiward and J. Gascoyne, modified with modern type and published in Walter Besant's London in the Time of the Tudors *(1904). The words 'The Posts of the Scaffold' appear rather indistinctly beneath the words Tower Hill.*

Reformation and the reintroduction of Roman Catholicism as the country's religion. Furthermore, her proposed marriage to Philip II of Spain was unpopular. A rebellion of some Protestant nobles was planned which, eventually, was led by Sir Thomas Wyatt (1521-1554). It was planned that four forces should descend on London from different directions, overwhelm the capital, capture Mary and place her half-sister, the future Elizabeth I, on the throne. In the event, only those forces belonging to Wyatt, whose power base was Kent, arrived with any numbers. They were barred from crossing London Bridge and instead marched west to Kingston, crossed the Thames there and then turned east again towards the City. On 6 February, Wyatt was prevented from entering London at Ludgate and he and his force were captured. As well as Wyatt, 90 collaborators were subsequently executed for treason. Further casualties by implication were Guilford Dudley and his wife, Lady Jane Grey, who had briefly usurped the throne before Mary became queen *(see Tower Green chapter)*. Wyatt, by then imprisoned in the White Tower, witnessed her execution six days after his arrest on Tower Green.

A contemporary report of his execution relates:

'The xjth of Aprell, being wenysdaye, was sir Thomas Wyat beheded upon Tower-hill. Before his coming downe out of the Tower, the lorde chamberlayne and the lorde Shandos caryed him to the tower over the Watergate, wher the lorde

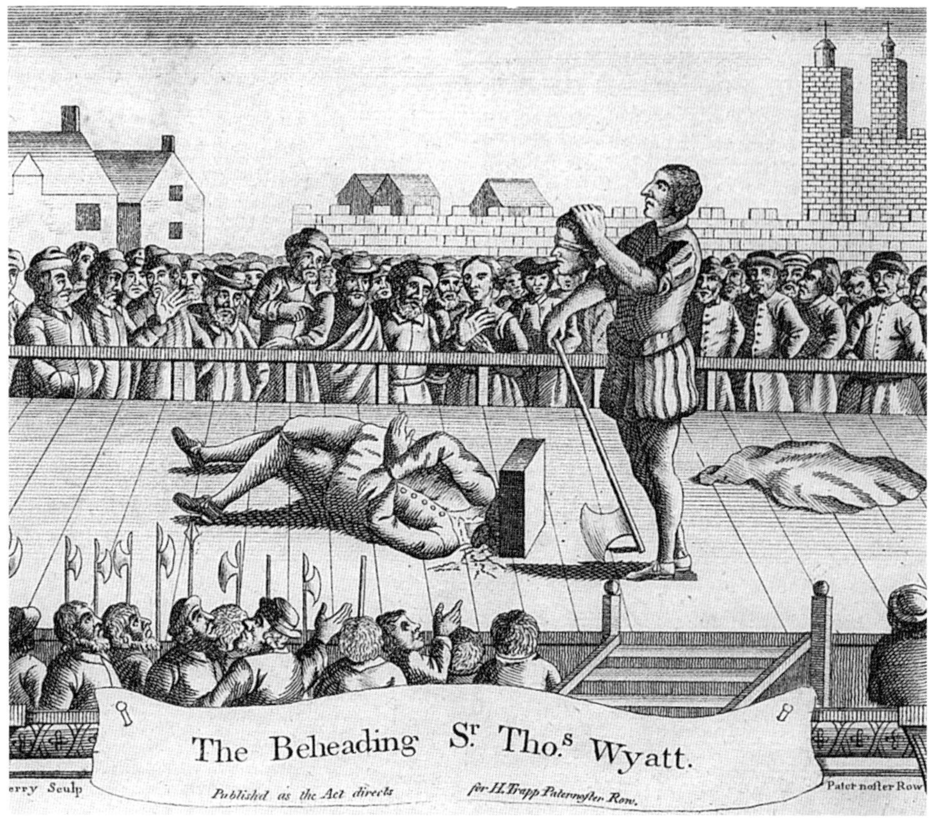

84. *The beheading of Sir Thomas Wyatt.*

Courtney laye, and ther he was before Courtney half an hower and more. What was spoken ys not yet knowen. Then he was brought out with a boke in his hande; and at the garden pale the lorde chamberlayne tooke his leave of him, and likewise master secretarye Bourne, to whom master Wyat said: "I praie you, sir, pray for me, and be a meane to the queen for my poore wife and children; and yf yt might have pleased her grace to have granted me my lyfe I wolde have trusted to have don hir such good service as shold have well recompenced myne offence; but, since not, I beseche God have mercy on me." To which master Bourne made no answer. So he cam toward the hill, Weston leading him by the one arme and the lorde Shandose by the other. When he was uppe apon the scaffolde he desired eche man to praye for him and with him and said these or moche-like words in effecte:

"Good people, I am come presently here to dye, being thereunto lawfully and wourthely condemned, for I have sorely offended against God and the qenes majestie, and am sorry therefore. I trust God hath forgiven and taken his mercy apon me. I besyche the queens majesty also of forgevenes." "She hath forgiven you allredy," saith Weston. "And let every man beware howe he taketh eny thinge in hande against the higher powers. Nlesse God be prosperable to his purpose, yt will never take good effecte or successe, and therof ye may now lerne at me. And I pray God I may be the last example in this place for that or eny other like. And whereas yt is said and wysled abroade, that I shoulde accuse my lady Elizabeth's grace, and my lorde Courtney; yt is not so, goode people, for I assure you neyther they nor eny other now. And whether Mr.Wyat, being then amased at such interruption, or whether they on the scaffold pluct him by the gown bake or no, yt is not well knowen, but without more talke he tourned him, and put of his gown and untrussyd his pointes;[3] then, taking the (earl of) Huntingdon, the lorde Hastinges, sir Giles Stranguesh, and many other by the handes, he plucked of his doblet and wastcote, unto his shirte, and knelyd downe upon the strawe, then laied his hed downe awhile, and rayse on his knees agayne, then after a few wourdes spoken, and his eyes lyft upp to heaven, he knytt the handekersheve himself about his eyes, and a lyttel holding upp his hands suddenly laid downe his hed, which the hangeman at one stroke toke from him. Then was he forthwith quarteryd apon the scaffold, and the next day his quarters set at diverse places, and his hed apon a stake apon the gallos beyond saynte James.[4] Which his hed, as ys reported, remained not there x.dayes unstolne awaye.'[5]

Wyatt's head was held up, and 'handekersheve' removed from the eyesto show the witnesses and crowd that the person that had died really was Wyatt. The body, as the report states, was quartered with one quarter being hung at Mile End Green, one at Newington, one at St Thomas of Waterings, and one near St.George's Church, Southwark. The head itself was mounted on a pole on the gallows which stood at Hay Hill between New Bond Street and Piccadilly. Rather curiously six days after the head had been placed on the gallows; it was stolen, probably by friends. It was never recovered.

Sir Henry Vane

Sir Henry Vane the Younger (1613-62), originally a Secretary of State to Charles I, became a leading Parliamentarian during the Commonwealth period, although he had no love of Cromwell's Protectorate. After the Restoration Vane had the dubious distinction of being one of twenty non-regicides excluded from the Act of Indemnity. In July 1660 a posse of soldiers marched to his house in Rosslyn Hill, Hampstead and there arrested him. He was then imprisoned for two years in the Scilly Isles, but then brought to the

85. The Earl of Strafford's execution on Tower Hill in 1641. Strafford had become increasingly unpopular with Parliament for his influence over the King and his unwise and unsuccessful military adventures. Charles cravenly gave in to Parliament and agreed to Strafford's trial and execution – which he much regretted and said so just before his own execution eight years later.

86. *Sir Henry Vane the Younger.*

Tower and on a trumped up charge put on trial. Charles II said that he was 'too dangerous a man to let live if we can honestly put him out of the way.' In June 1662 he was tried for high treason. During the course of his trial he asserted his belief in the supreme power of Parliament.

Vane was a man of courage and independence of mind and his execution was one that derived from his criticism of the government of Charles II. Vane, a committed republican, was not afraid to speak his mind and the scaffold gave Vane the opportunity of a final speech which, the authorities feared, might demean the king. The *State Trials* account of the proceedings show a strong God-fearing man, who believed that his impending death would unite him with his God. Charles II commuted his original sentence of death by hanging at Tyburn, to the more appropriate punishment of beheading on Tower Hill. He was allowed the further privilege of having his relatives give his head and body a decent private interment. The accounts of the execution illustrate its political nature and the methods used to suppress any anti-monarchical speech. The Sheriff specifically requested Vane to hold his tongue:

> 'Then Mr. Sheriff coming into the room, was friendly saluted by him [Vane], and after a little pause communicated a prohibition that he said he had received, which was, That he must not speak any thing against his majesty or the government. His answer to this he himself relates on the Scaffold. He further told Mr. Sheriff, he was ready; but the Sheriff said he was not, nor could be this half hour yet....'[6]

Vane asked to have his servants attend him on the scaffold, and that they should be well-treated. The Sheriff agreed, but at the scaffold a little later they were forcibly restrained from attending him. It was also agreed that he could walk in a dignified way from his cell to Tower Hill, but a sledge, a demeaning form of transport, arrived to take him. Both these setbacks indicate an attempt to reduce his stature to the onlookers. When the sledge arrived 'he went very cheerfully and readily down the stairs from his chamber, and seating himself on the sledge ... he was forthwith drawn away towards the Scaffold.' His popularity is clear from the reception given by the crowd during the short journey to Tower Hill where he was greeted and shouted at by well-wishers. He in return repeatedly took off his hat and bowed to the crowd ...

> '... being passed within the rails on Tower-Hill, there were loud acclamations of the people, crying out, The Lord Jesus go with your dear soul, &c.'[7]

He arrived cheerfully at the scaffold, and pushed his way through the crowds in order to ascend. So confused was the scene that the crowd was uncertain which person was Vane.

'The prisoner thereupon, stepped forward, saluted the multitude on each side of the scaffold with his hat off, and then returned to his company.'[8]

He then addressed the crowd claiming that the proceedings against him were wrong at which point the Sheriff, Sir John Robinson, told him that 'he lied.' Vane replied that 'God will judge between me and you. I speak but matter of fact ...' The attending drummers and trumpeters then drowned him out on the two succeeding parts of his speech which were deemed offensive to the crown, 'and, at length, after various interruptions of the same kind, and after several attempts had been made to snatch away the paper which he held in his hand, he tore his notes in pieces, and prepared for the block.'[9]

Pepys was there, of course.

'Up by four o'clock in the morning and upon business at my office. Then we sat down to business, and about 11 o'clock, having a room got ready for us, we all went out to the Tower-hill; and there, over against the scaffold, made on purpose this day, saw Sir Henry Vane brought. A very great press of people. He made a long speech, many times interrupted by the Sheriff and others there; and they would have taken his paper out of his hand, but he would not let it go. But they caused all the books of those that writ after him to be given the Sheriff; and the trumpets were brought under the scaffold that he might not be heard. Then he prayed, and so fitted himself, and received the blow; but the scaffold was so crowded that we could not see it done. But Boreman, who had been upon the scaffold, came to us and told us, that first he began to speak of the irregular proceeding against him; that he was, against Magna Charta, denied to have his exceptions against the indictment allowed; and that there he was stopped by the Sheriff. Then he drew out his, paper of notes, and begun to tell them first his life; that he was born a gentleman, that he was bred up and had the quality of a gentleman, and to make him in the opinion of the world more a gentleman, he had been, till he was seventeen years old, a good fellow, but then it pleased God to lay a foundation of grace in his heart, by which he was persuaded, against his worldly interest, to leave all preferment and go abroad, where he might serve God with more freedom. Then he was called home, and made a member of the Long Parliament; where he never did, to this day, any thing against his conscience, but all for the glory of God. Here he would have given them an account of the proceedings of the Long Parliament, but they so often interrupted him, that at last he was forced to give over: and so fell into prayer for England in generall, then for the churches in England, and then for the City of London: and so fitted himself for the block, and received the blow.

He had a blister, or issue, upon his neck, which he desired them not hurt: he changed not his colour or speech to the last, but died justifying himself and the cause he had stood for; and spoke very confidently of his being presently at the right hand of Christ; and in all, things appeared the most resolved man that ever died in that manner, and showed more of heat than cowardize, but yet with all humility and gravity. One asked him why he did not pray for the King. He answered, "Nay," says he, "you shall see I can pray for the King: I pray God bless him!" The King had given his body to his friends; and, therefore, he told them that he hoped they would be civil to his body when dead; and desired they would let him die like a gentleman and a Christian, and not crowded and pressed as he was.'

More mundanely, Pepys continues:

'So to the office a little, and so to the Trinity-house all of us to dinner; and then to the office again all the afternoon till night. So home and to bed.'

James, Duke of Monmouth

Monmouth (1649-85) was a son of Charles II by his mistress Lucy Walter. He had no recognised claim to the throne on the death of his father, though he always alleged that Charles had secretly married his mother. However, the unpopularity of James II, Catholic brother of Charles, persuaded him to lead a rebellion in

87. *James, Duke of Monmouth.*

88. *The execution of the Duke of Monmouth after his failed rebellion.*

1685, about six months after the accession of James. It was put down at the Battle of Sedgemoor, near Bridgewater, on 6 July and the event is chiefly remembered for the brutality of the notorious Judge Jeffreys who sentenced 320 persons to death, and 800 to transportation in a series of trials which had little to do with justice.[10]

Roberts in his two-volume work on Monmouth, the rebellion and subsequent execution claims to draw his report of the demise of the Duke on Tower Hill from a 'very scarce sheet of four folio pages, printed at the time by authority.'[11] It was entitled, he wrote,

> 'An Account of what passed at the Execution of the late Duke of Monmouth, on Wednesday the 15th of July, 1685, on Tower Hill; together with a Paper signed by himself that Morning in the Tower, in the Presence of the Lords Bishops of Ely and Bath and Wells, Dr. Tennison, and Dr. Hooper.'

Roberts notes that 'The lieutenant brought him [Monmouth] some steps without the fortress in his coach, and then delivered him to the sheriffs of the city, who conducted him on foot through a hedge of soldiery, accompanied by three officers with pistols in their hands, and

who ascended the scaffold with him, and remained near him till the execution. Another source referred to by Roberts says that 'on Monmouth's first appearance a murmur of sighs and groans went round the whole assembly, which by degrees sank into a breathless silence, as if every syllable he had to utter was sacred, and not to be profaned with the unhallowed mixture of any vulgar sound.' James II made a concession to his nephew by allowing the scaffold to be draped in black for mourning, and allowing his body to be given to friends to be 'disposed of as they shall think fit.' The following description of the execution seems authentic as opposed to many politically motivated reports. Some non-relevant sections have been removed.

'The late Duke of Monmouth came from the Tower to the Scaffold, at Ten, A.M., Wednesday, 15th July, attended by the Bishop of Ely, the Bishop of Bath and Wells, Dr. Tennison, and Dr. Hooper, which four the King was graciously pleased to send him, as his Assistants, to prepare him for Death; and the late Duke himself intreated all four of them to accompany him to the Place of Execution, and to continue with him to the last. The two Bishops, going in the Lieutenant's Coach with him to the Bars, made seasonable and devout Applications to him all the way ; and one of them desired him not to be surprised if they, to the very last, upon the Scaffold, renewed those Exhortations to a Particular Repentance, which they had so often repeated before. At his first coming upon the Scaffold he looked for the Executioner, and seeing him, said, "Is this the man to do the business? Do your work well." 'Then the late Duke of Monmouth began to speak, [to] some one or other of the Assistants, during the whole time, applying themselves to him. There then followed a long battle of words between Monmouth and those appointed to attend him. They repeatedly urged him to confess and repent his rebellion, which he declined to do and referred them to a paper he had written on the matter.

Monmouth. I shall say but very little: I come to die : I die a Protestant of the Church of England.

Assistant. My Lord, if you be of the Church of England, you must acknowledge the Doctrine of Non-resistance to be true?

Monmouth. If I acknowledge the Doctrine of the Church of England in general, that includes all.

Monmouth then raised the matter of his relationship with Lady Henrietta Wentworth.

Assistant. In your Opinion, perhaps, Sir, as you have been told [i.e. in the Tower] but this is not fit Discourse in this Place.

Mr. Sheriff Gostlin. Sir, were you ever married to her?

Monmouth. This is not a Time to Answer that Question.

Mr. Sheriff Gostlin. Sir, I hoped to have heard of your Repentance for the Treason and Bloodshed which have been committed.

Monmouth. I dy very penitent.

Assistant. My Lord, It is fit to be Particular; and, considering the Publick Evil you have done, you ought to do as much good now as possibly you can, by a Publick acknowledgement.

Monmouth. What I have thought fit to say of Publick affairs is in a Paper which I have signed. I refer to my Paper.

And later:

Monmouth. I repent of all things that a true Christian ought to repent of. I am to die. Pray, Mr. Lord.

Assistant. Then (My Lord) we can only recommend you to the Mercy of God; but we cannot pray with that Chearfulness and Encouragement as we should if you had made a Particular Acknowledgement.

And then again:

Monmouth. I am sorry for invading the Kingdom and for the Blood that has been shed; and for the Souls which may have been lost by my means. I am sorry it ever happened (which he spake softly).

Mr. Sheriff Vandeput [to some that stood at a distance] He says he is very sorry for invading the Kingdom.

Assistant. God Almighty of his infinite Mercy forgive you. Here are great numbers of spectators;

here are the Sheriff's; they represent the Great City; and in speaking to them, you speak to a whole City : make some Satisfaction by owning your Crime before them.

'He was silent here. Then all went to solemn Commendatory Prayers, which continued for a good space; the late Duke of Monmouth and the Company kneeling, and joining in them with great fervency. Prayers being ended, before he, and the four who assisted him, were risen from their knees, he was again earnestly exhorted to a true and thorough Repentance. After they were risen up, he was exhorted to pray for the King; and was asked, Whether he did not desire to send some dutiful Message to His MAJESTY, and to recommend his Wife and Children to his Majesty's Favour.'

Monmouth. What harm have they done? Do it, if you please; I pray for him and for all men.

Assistant. My Lord, you have been bred a Souldier: you will do a generous Christian thing, if you please to go to the Bail, and speak to the Souldiers, and say that here you stand, a sad example of Rebellion, and entreat them and the People to be Loyal and Obedient to the King.

Monmouth. I have said I will make no Speeches: I will make no Speeches : I come to die.

Assistant. My Lord, ten words will be enough.

Monmouth. (Then calling his Servant, and giving him something like a Toothpick-Case) Here (said he), give this to the Person to whom you are to deliver the other things.

Monmouth. (To the executioner) Here are six guineas for you : pray do your business well : do not serve me as you did my Lord Russell. I have heard you struck him three or four times. Here (to his servant), take these remaining guineas, and give them to him, if he does his work well.

Executioner. I hope I shall.

Monmouth. If you strike me twice, I cannot promise you not to stir. Prithee let me feel the axe: (he felt the edge, and said), I fear it is not sharp enough.

Executioner. It is sharp enough and heavy enough.

Then he lay down again.

It is probably understandable that the authorities do not refer to one of the worst decapitations undertaken at Tower Hill. It has been reported that the executioner's nerves were so bad that he 'was much more agitated than he who was to suffer.'

A contemporary German pamphlet provides an account of the remaining events of that day:

'...the botcherly dog, the executioner, did so barbarously act his pairt, that he could not at fyve stroaks of the ax sever the head from the body." At the first, which made only a slight dash in his neck, his [Monmouth's] body heaved up and his head turned about; the second stroke made only a deeper dash, after which the body moved; the third not doing the work, he threw away the axe, and said "God damme, I can doe no more, my heart fails me." The executioner declared that his limbs were stiffened, (probably paralysed with fear) and that he would willingly give forty guineas to any one who would finish the work. The bystanders had much ado to forbear throwing him over the scaffold ; but made him take the axe again, threatening to kill him if he did not do his duty better. With two strokes more, not being able to finish the work, he was fain to draw forth his long knife, and with it to cut off the remaining part of his neck. He could not hold the head: he only showed it once to the people. If there had been no guard before the soldiers, to conduct the executioner away, the people would have torn him to pieces, so great was their indignation at the barbarous usage of the late Duke of Monmouth at his hands. After his death, the people ran in crowds to the scaffold, and dipped, some their handkerchiefs and some their shirts, in his blood, as it is the custom to do on such occasions, notwithstanding the danger from the thrusts of the halberts and pikes, which they carried away as a precious relic.'

Immediately after his death Monmouth's head was re-attached to the body, in order to allow a portrait to be drawn. He was placed in a black velvet covered coffin which stood waiting on the scaffold and driven to St. Peter ad Vincula at the Tower in a six-horse mourning coach. The body was then interred under the communion table of the chapel.

William Boyd, 4th Earl of Kilmarnock
The trial of William Boyd for high treason in 1746 was remarkable for a semblance of fairness offered to the Scottish peers. He and a number of other Scottish nobles who were part of the Jacobite Rebellion, were captured after the Battle of Culloden in April 1746 and brought to London.

The execution on Tower Hill was unusual in that a scaffold was erected adjoining number 14 Tower Hill, against a house in which the earl, and his fellow peer in misfortune, Lord Balmerino, were to wait until everything was ready. The two men walked from the Tower, where they were both being held, and in the house prepared for their executions in an almost leisurely and relaxed manner. The executions reflect the protocols and etiquette of the scaffold of the time. On being informed of his execution, to take place the following Monday, 'Lord Kilmarnock received this news with the outward behaviour of a man, that knew and felt the importance of the scene of death, but without any marks of disorder, without any unbecoming anxiousness or terror.'[12] The Sheriff, who brought the news to the earl, out of sympathy for Kilmarnock warned him of the nature of the ordeal he was about to undergo in order to allow him to prepare himself:

> '....I told him, That all mankind were really under sentence of death, though they knew not the manner or precise time when it would be executed; it might be to any one as soon or sooner than his own; that they not expecting it, nor having such timely and certain notice of it, might die wholly unguarded and unprepared; while he had warning, and the most awakening motives to fit himself in the best manner possible for this grand and decisive event.'

The earl answered that he was a good Christian and had, as such, no fear concerning

89. The Lords Kilmarnock and Balmerino and a fanciful depiction of their execution.

death, indeed 'he thought it a trifle' and with regard to the mechanism of his death he had 'no great reason to be terrified, for that the stroke [of the axe] appeared to be scarce so much as the pain of drawing a tooth or the first shock of the cold bath upon a weak and fearful temper.' The Sheriff, Williamson, obviously had empathy and respect for the earl and engaged in some gentle psychotherapy to prepare Kilmarnock for what awaited him. He did not want him to show any involuntary shock.

The under-sheriff noted that Williamson, on the Saturday preceding the execution, 'gave him a minute detail of all the circumstances of solemnity and outward terror that would accompany it, and that he 'heard it with ... much shew of composure ...

> 'He was told, That on Monday, about ten in the morning, the sheriffs would come to demand the prisoners, who would deliver them at the gate of the Tower; that from thence, if their lordships

90. Plaque commemorating the Lords Kilmarnock and Balmerino on Tower Hill, 2007.

thought proper, they should walk on foot to the house appointed on Tower-hill for their reception, where the rooms would be hung with black, to make the more decent and solemn appearance, and that the scaffold also would be covered with black cloth; that his lordship might repose and prepare himself, in the room fitted up for him, as long as he thought it convenient, remembering only, that the warrant for the execution was limited to, and consequently expired at one o' clock; that because of a complaint made by the lord Kenmure, that the block was too low, it was ordered to be raised to the height of two feet; that it might be the more firmly fixed, props would be placed directly under it, that the certainty or decency of the execution might not be obstructed by any concussion, or sudden jerk of the body. All this lord Kilmarnock, without the least visible emotion, expressed his satisfaction in: but when the general told him, that two mourning hearses would be provided, and placed close by the scaffold, that when the head was struck of, the coffins might soon be taken out to receive the bodies; he said, That he thought it would be better for the coffin to be upon the scaffold, for by that means the bodies would be still sooner removed out of sight.

Once on the scaffold, Kilmarnock embraced his friends, and took his leave of them. He was then 'introduced' to the executioner who asked his forgiveness for the 'painful task allotted to him.'

Horace Walpole commented that the executioner was dressed in white with a white apron and out of 'tenderness' concealed the axe behind him. One account says that when Kilmarnock 'beheld the fatal scaffold covered with black cloth; the executioner with his axe and his assistants; the saw-dust, which was soon to be drenched with his blood; the coffin prepared to receive the limbs which were yet warm with life; above all, the immense display of human countenances which surrounded the scaffold like a sea, all eyes being bent on the sad object of the preparation, – his natural feelings broke forth in a whisper to the friend on whose arm he leaned, "Home, this is terrible!"[13] He then handed the executioner a purse containing payment, and gave him final instructions: he was to wait for the signal which would be when he dropped his handkerchief. Kilmarnock's servants then helped him to take his coat off, and place his hair under a cap, 'lest the blow be intercepted' after which, with total composure he knelt down at the block and proceeded to pray for about six minutes. He then dropped the handkerchief, on which the headsman struck, decapitating him with one blow. The head was placed in a piece of scarlet baize and then into the waiting coffin along with his body. It was then handed over to friends.

Walpole's[14] account depicts a slightly less composed version of the execution. He comments that when Kilmarnock came to the scaffold although he was resolute he was also 'much terrified'. When the earl after 'testing' the block several times knelt down at the block he showed a 'visible unwillingness to depart' taking five minutes to drop the handkerchief, which was his signal to the executioner to strike.

With the death of his friend, Lord Kilmarnock, it was then the turn of Lord Balmerino. The under-sheriff went to the house. As he entered Balmerino said to him 'I suppose my lord

Kilmarnock is no more?' He then asked how well the executioner had performed, and on being told said 'then it was well; and now, gentlemen I will detain you no longer for I desire not to protract my life.' An eyewitness reports that:

'His lordship then observing the executioner with the axe in his hand, took it from him, and having felt the edge, returned it him again, at the same time shewing him where to strike the blow, and animating him to do it with resolution; "For in that, friend," (said his lordship) "will consist your mercy."

Unfortunately for Balmerino the executioner took two blows of the axe:

'...the executioner was so terrified at his lordship's intrepidity, and the suddenness of the signal, that notwithstanding he struck his lordship in the part directed, yet the force of the blow was not sufficient to sever the head from the body, though (happily) sufficient to deprive him of all sensation.'

The observer continues to describe in detail what then happened:

'...After the first blow, his lordship's head fell back upon his shoulders, but being afterward severed at two more gentle blows, was then received into a piece of red baize, and with his body deposited in his coffin, and delivered to his friends.'[15]

Chambers' *Book of Days* (1869) notes that the house:

'....still exists, marked as No. 14 Tower Hill. The two lords were in succession led out of this house on to the scaffold, Kilmarnock suffering before Balmerino, in melancholy reference to his higher rank in the peerage. Their mutilated bodies, after being deposited in their respective coffins, are said to have been brought back into the house, and in proof of this, a trail of blood is still visible along the hall and up the first flight of stairs. There is a contemporary print of the execution, representing the scaffold as surrounded by a wide square of dragoons, beyond which are great multitudes of people, many of them seated in wooden galleries. The decapitated lords were all respectfully buried in St. Peter's Chapel within the Tower.'

91. Simon Fraser, 11th Baron Lovat. the last person to be beheaded on Tower Hill.

Simon Fraser, 11th Lord Lovat

Lovat (*c*.1667-April 9 1747) was a colourful character who led a turbulent life. Having initially been a supporter of the Hanoverian succession, in 1745 he changed his mind to support the Stuart claim to the crown of Scotland. The Jacobite cause was defeated at the Battle of Culloden on 16 April, 1746, but it was some time before Fraser was captured, hiding in a hollow tree, and brought to London for trial for high treason. He conducted himself in 1747 with a

92. The trial of Lord Lovat at Westminster Hall.

certain levity which is noted in a number of contemporary sources as though Lovat was not taking his impending fate seriously.

> 'The conduct of Lovat at his trial and execution was most extraordinary. When a principal witness had given in his testimony upon which depended the issue of the trial, the defendant being asked if he had any question to propose to the witness, replied, "I only wish him joy of his young wife:" and after sentence of death had been pronounced against him – in the horrible terms in which sentences for treason are delivered – as he was retiring, he called out, "Fare you well, my lords: we shall not all meet again in one place." At the execution, however, he indulged in no offensive levity, but behaved with great propriety, calling out just at last, *Dulce et decorum est pro patria mori*." It is glorious to die for one's country.'

State Trials and Proceedings offers the reader 'An account of the behaviour of Simon Lord Lovat, from the time his death-warrant was delivered, to the day of his execution. By a Gentleman who attended his Lordship in his last moments.'[16] Lovat, well aware that his behaviour after the trial and at the execution would be the subject of scrutiny, would have wanted to leave a good impression. *State Trials* tells us that on Friday, 3 April, when the messenger bearing the warrant for his execution arrived, Lovat 'thanked him kindly for the favour ... and assured him he was well satisfied with his doom ...'[17] On that same day, he is described as smoking his pipe and being 'very cheerful.' He refers to his portliness – as depicted in his caricature by Hogarth – as causing problems for the executioner. In fact a special 'engine' was being prepared to take account of the problem. He said that 'as his neck was very short, the executioner would be puzzled to find it out with his axe; and if such a machine was made, they might call it Lord Lovat's Maiden."[18] We are also told that contrary to popular belief, Lovat was not a drunkard as he 'never drank more than two pints of wine a day ... and never any without water.' On the Thursday of his execution,

> 'his lordship awaked about three o'clock in the morning, and prayed most devoutly. At five he

got up, called for a glass of wine and water, according to his usual custom, and seemed still as cheerful as ever; then being placed in his chair, sat and read till seven, when he called for another glass of wine and water. About eight o'clock he desired Mr. Sherrington, one of the warders, to send his wig that the barber might have time to comb it out. He then called for a purse to put his money in for the executioner, and desired it might be a good one, lest the gentleman should refuse it. Mr. Southbey, one of his lordship's warders, I remember, brought him two purses, the one a green silk knit, and the other a yellow canvass, but which his lordship made choice of I really forget; however, it was a purse, as he observed, that no man would dislike with ten guineas in it ... As his lordship was now within a few hours of death and had behaved with such surprising intrepidity during his whole confinement, I was the more particular in observing every little incident that happened. But though he had a great share of memory and understanding ... His behaviour was all of a piece, and he was the same facetious companion now, as he was before sentence was passed against him ...'

In a parody which borders on studied nonchalance, again probably with an eye to future chroniclers, he commented that his barber had brought his wig and had not powdered it on account of it being a rainy day. His attending companion reports:

'He seemed angry, and said, "That he went to the block with pleasure, and he had a suit of velvet embroidered, he would wear it on that occasion."'

In conversation with his barber, he remarked that he would be in heaven by one o' clock which was his reason for being so happy. Impending doom did little to constrain his Lordship's appetite. At 9.30 a couple of hours before his execution 'his lordship called for a plate of minced veal, eat[en] very heartily ... he then called for some wine and water, and drank the healths of several of his friends.' It was then, at 10 am while Lovat was taking his final drinks in the Tower, that with crowds gathering on Tower Hill in large numbers the grandstand collapsed:

'At ten a terrible accident happened upon the hill, by the fall of a scaffold, which put all the people in great confusion; several persons were killed, and numbers maimed and bruised.'

It was shortly after this incident that the sheriffs of London called for Lovat who asked for a short time to pray, and then said that he was ready. As an ill, corpulent 80-year-old man, he proceeded very slowly down the stairs in the Tower maintaining an air of politeness, but complaining that the stairs were 'very troublesome to him.'

'When he came to the door, he bowed to the people, and he was then put into the governor's coach, and carried to the outer gate where he was taken out of the governor's coach, and delivered to the sheriffs of the city of London and county of Middlesex, who conducted him in another coach to a house near the scaffold which had been lined in black cloth for his lordship's reception...'

The civilised, social manner of the process of execution is emphasised when Lovat requested of the sheriffs that he might have the favour of being attended by his friends and relatives. These were allowed into the house. In return for this favour Lovat informed the sheriffs that 'It was a considerable consolation to him that his body fell into the hands of gentlemen of so much honour ...' and, he then added, as if to dispel any concerns of that nature that, 'I will give you, gentlemen, and the government no farther trouble, for I shall make no speech; though I have a paper to leave, with which you may do as you think proper.'[19] Lovat then said further prayers after which the sheriff asked him 'if he would refresh himself with a glass of wine?' Lovat replied that he would take some 'burnt brandy and bitters'. Lovat, as if attending a genteel social occasion then turned to the sheriff during which a civilised conversation of a practical

93. *The official site of the scaffold at Tower Hill. The view of the Tower which lies to the right behind the War Memorial is obscured. The plaque in the centre is shown enlarged below (94).*

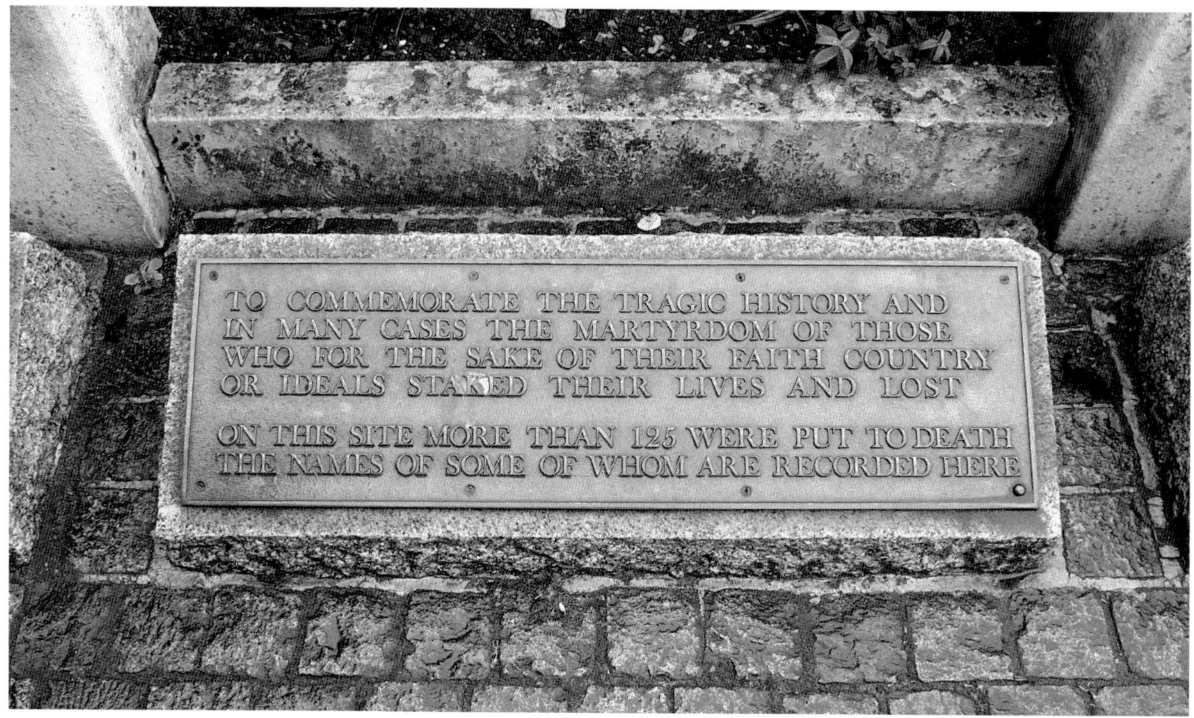

95. The execution block on display in the Tower that was used at and probably made for the execution of Lord Lovat.

95a. The block. Clearly visible on the top are the grooves where the axe fell.

nature took place and he informed the sheriff that 'He was ready to go whenever he pleased,' to which the sheriff replied:

'My Lord ... I would not hurry your lordship', and taking out his watch, said, 'There is half an hour good, if your lordship don't tarry too long upon the scaffold.' Lovat then desired that his clothes might be delivered to his friends with his corpse, and not given to the executioner, and said, 'For that reason he should give him [the executioner] ten guineas.' He then asked, if he might have the axe brought him to feel if it was sharp, and desired that his head, when taken off, might be received in a cloth, and put into the coffin.[20]

The sheriff, mindful of the original sentence that Lovat should have been hanged, drawn and quartered, conferred with some gentlemen present and commented that he had

'...received a warrant in the usual form for the execution of his lordship, and as it had not been customary of late years to expose the head at the four corners of the scaffold, he really thought he might indulge his lordship with a promise as to that point, for he did not think he could expose the head (though it was desired, and indeed ordered by a message) without being liable to censure;" adding withal, "That he was truly sensible of the duty he owed his majesty, and should always pay a great regard to the orders he received from his grace the duke of Newcastle, or any of his ministry." And then turning to his lordship, told him, "That what he desired should be punctually observed."'[21]

With the assistance of two gentlemen, Lovat then proceeded to the scaffold. On going up the steps he looked around him and said, "God save us! Why should there be such a bustle about taking off an old grey head that cannot get up three steps without two men to support it?" In contrast to the rough and tumble mob of Tyburn, a low key protocol unfolded on Tower Hill. The same gentleman who had accompanied Lovat from the time of his condemnation reports:

'The first person he sought when he came upon the scaffold was the executioner, who was immediately presented to him; and after he had made his obeisance, my lord put his hand into his pocket, and pulled out a purse with ten guineas, saying, "Here, Sir, is ten guineas for you, pray do your work well; for if you should cut and hack my shoulders, and I should be able to rise again, I shall be very angry with you."

Lovat looked at his coffin, on which was written, Simon Dominus Fraser de Lovat, decolat. April 9, 1747, AEtat suae, 80. He then sat down again, and repeated a following line out of Horace:

"Dulce et decorum est pro Patria mori."

("Tis a glorious sad pleasant thing to die for our country.")

He then called for Mr. William Fraser, his solicitor and agent in Scotland, and holding up his gold-headed cane, said, 'I deliver you this cane in token of my sense of your faithful services, and of my committing to you all the power I have upon earth'. He then took off his wig, ordered his cap to be put on, and after taking off some clothes, knelt down to the block, took hold of the cloth which was placed to receive his head and pulled it close to him. He dropped his handkerchief when he was ready and the executioner severed his head with one blow.

[1] Walter Thornbury, *Old and New London*, Vol. 2 (1878), pp. 95-100.

[2] *Ibid*, pp. 117-21.

[3] Unfastened the lace that secured his doublet

[4] It is possible that this is a reference to the gallows at Charing Cross

[5] J.G. Nichols, *et al.*, *The Chronicle of Queen Jane, and of two years of Queen Mary, and especially of the rebellion of Sir Thomas Wyat, Written by a Resident in the Tower of London*, pp 72-74

[6] State Trials, p. 191

[7] *Ibid*, p. 191

[8] Clayton, J. W. (1859). *Personal Memoirs of Charles the Second; with sketches of his court and times.* 2 vols. (C. J. Skeet: London, 1859), p. 163

[9] *Ibid*, p. 165

[10] G. Roberts, *The Life, Progresses, and Rebellion of James, Duke of Monmouth, to his capture and execution: with a full account of the Bloody Assize, and copious biographical notices*, 2 vols. (1844).

[11] *Ibid*, p. 142

[12] *Ibid*, pp 142-152

[13] Proceedings against the Earl of Kilmarnock, from *A Complete Collection of State Trials* (1828) p. 508

[14] W. S. Scott, *Tales of a grandfather*. (Edinburgh, 1849). Quoted from p. 53 of Walpole's *Letters*.

[15] Horace Walpole, *The letters of Horace Walpole*. (1891), pp. 53-54

[16] *State Trials*, Vol. VIII, Howell pp. 442-530

[17] *Ibid*, pp. 853-854.

[18] A reference to a guillotine type construction in use at the time in the north.

[19] *Ibid*, p. 842

[20] *Ibid*, p. 852

[21] *Ibid*, p. 852

CHAPTER TEN

Lincoln's Inn Fields

It is difficult to imagine on a sunny spring day when this square is packed with suited men and women enjoying the pleasant aspect of Lincoln's Inn for lunch and a peaceful break, that this was once a place of execution

William, Lord Russell

In the vicinity of the bandstand, on 21 July 1683, Lord Russell (1639-1683), a son of the 5th earl and later the first Duke of Bedford, was executed after being implicated in the Rye House Plot, which planned to assassinate both Charles II and his brother, the future James II, on their way back from Newmarket - Rye House, owned by a Republican, was in Hoddesdon.

An early suggestion was that Russell should be executed in front of his own house, Southampton House, facing what is now Bloomsbury Square, but the king thought this indecent and nearby Lincoln's Inn Fields was decided upon. On his way to execution as his carriage turned into Little Queen Street, just off what became part of Kingsway in the vicinity of Lincoln's Inn, he shed a tear 'at the remembrance of his wife....'[1] Bishop Burnet wrote:

96. William, Lord Russell.

> 'Tillotson and I went with him in the coach to the place of execution. Some of the crowd that filled the streets wept, while others insulted. He was touched by the tenderness that the one gave him, but did not seem at all provoked by the other. He was singing psalms a great part of the way, and said he hoped to sing better soon. As he observed the great crowds of people all the way he said to us, "I hope I shall quickly see a much better assembly." When he came to the scaffold he walked about it four or five times. Then he turned to the sheriffs and delivered his paper. He protested that he had always been far from any designs on the King's life or government. ... He prayed God would preserve both, and the Protestant religion. In his he owned he had a great zeal against Popery, which he looked on as an idolatrous and bloody religion, but that, although he was at all times ready to venture his life for his religion or his country, yet this would never have carried him to any black or wicked design. He concluded with some very devout ejaculations. After he had delivered this paper, he prayed by himself; then Tillotson prayed with him. After that, he prayed again by himself, and then

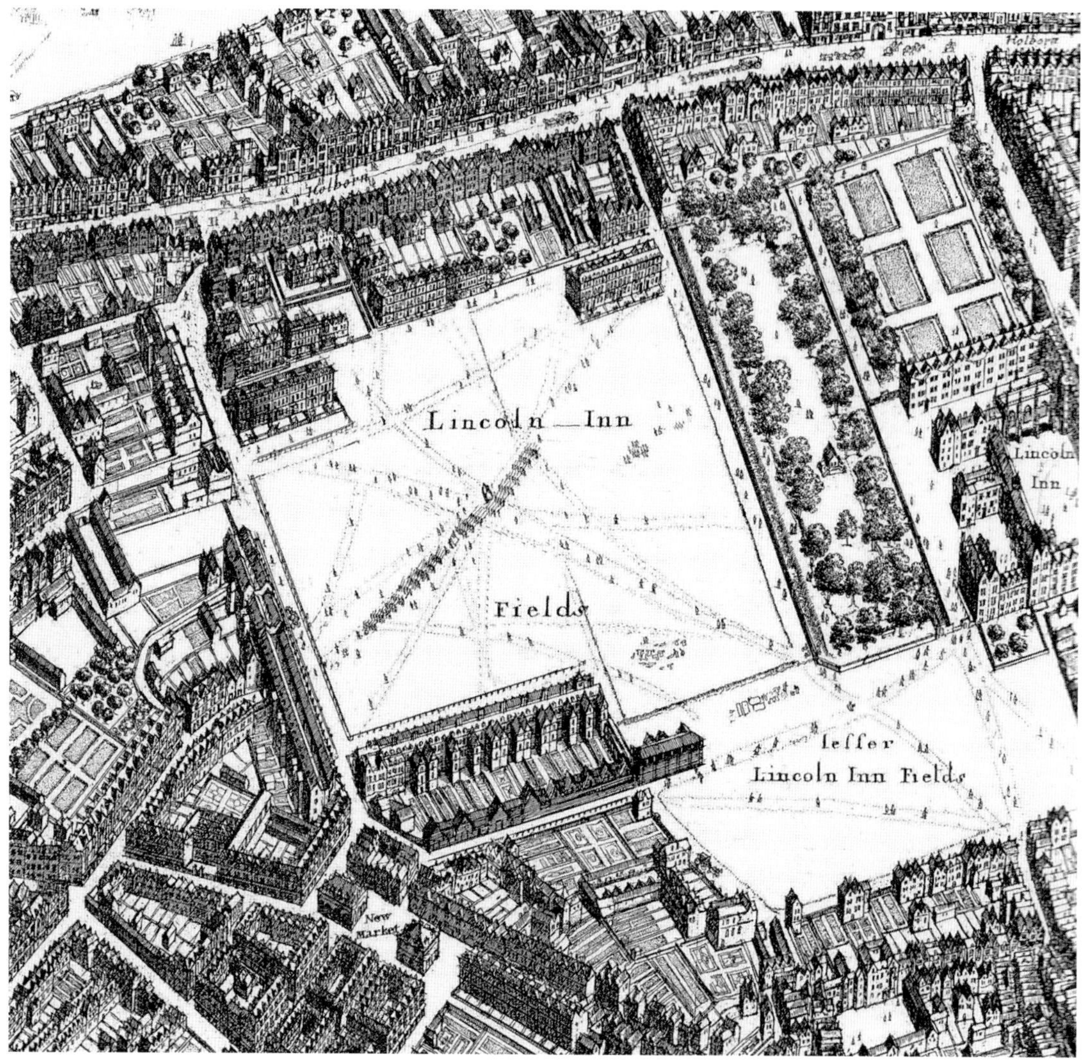

97. *Lincoln's Inn Fields in the 1650s.*

> undressed himself, and laid his head on the block, without the least change of countenance; and it was cut off at two strokes."[2]

What Burnet omitted to mention to the King was that the executioner, Jack Ketch, made such a poor job of the decapitation that four axe blows were required. After the first stroke, Russell looked up and said to executioner 'You dog, did I give you 10 guineas to use me so inhumanely?' Five years later when the Duke of Monmouth mounted the scaffold at Tower Hill, and realised he had the same executioner he asked Ketch if he thought the axe was sharp enough, handed him 6 guineas, and promised him a further sum if he did his work properly, commenting:

"Pray do not serve me as you did my Lord Russell. I have heard you struck him four or five times; If you strike me twice, I cannot promise you not to stir."

An inscription once stood on the place of execution which read: 'On this spot was

98. St Michael's church, Chenies, Bucks.

99. The bandstand in Lincoln's Inn Fields, believed to be near the site of the execution of Lord Russell.

100. The Bedford family mausoleum in St Michael's church.

beheaded, William, Lord Russell, a lover of constitutional liberty 21st July AD 1683'. The plaque is no longer there, but it was probably in the vicinity of the bandstand.[3]

Russell's body lies in the Bedford family mausoleum in St Michael's Church, Chenies in Buckinghamshire near Amersham.

1 John Smith and Charles Mackay, *Streets of London*, (1861 edn) p .185

2 Bishop Burnet's report to Charles II on the execution, taken from Smith and Mackay

3 I am grateful to Diane Burstein for this information.

CHAPTER ELEVEN

St Paul's Churchyard

The Gunpowder Plot conspirators

The Gunpowder Plot was discovered on 5 November 1605 and the conspirators were executed, some here at St Paul's, some at Westminster, in the following January. The illustration of the *Weekely News* reproduced here, reporting the executions, is a much later, probably 19th-century, rendering of the original, judging by its precise type face and the fact that the date has been translated to what we now regard as 1606 but was then, under the old style dating system, still 1605.

The accused are referred to as 'the eight papists ... monsters in nature...' Of the offence itself the *Weekely Newes* describes it apoplectically as '... so odious in the ears of all human creatures that it could hardly be believed that so many monsters in nature should carry the shapes of men – murder!' The plotters were held at the Tower and tried at Westminster. The four to die at St Paul's were Everard Digby, the elder Winter, Grant and Bates. Following sentence they were taken back to the Tower and on 27 January 1606 were 'drawn upon sledges and hurdles into

101. Plan of St Paul's Churchyard from Leake's Survey of the Post-Fire City (1667). The Gunpowder Plot conspirators and Father Garnet were executed on the north-western side where one of the alleyways leads into Paternoster Row.

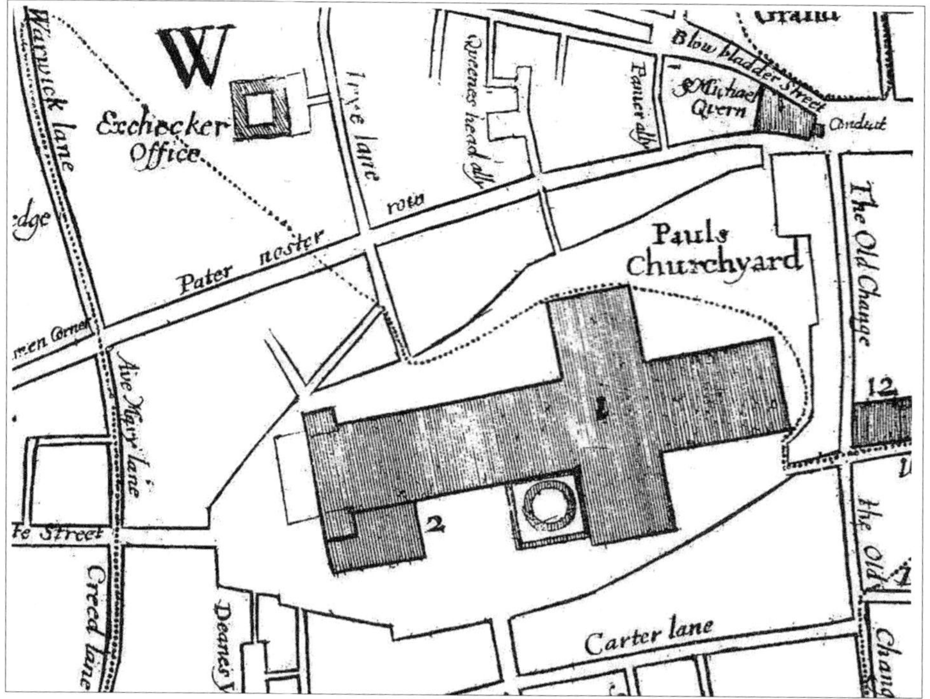

THE — Numb. 19.

WEEKELY NEWES.

London: Printed for Jeffrey Chorlton, and are to be Sold at his Shop, at the great North Door of St. Paul's, 1606.—Munday, 31st January, 1606.

A Brief Discourse upon the Arraignment and Execution of the eight traytors—Digby, the two Winters, Graunt, Rookewood, Keyes, Bates, and Johnson, alias Guy Fawkes, four of which were executed in St. Paul's Churchyard, in London, upon Thursday, the 27th last, the other four in the Old Palace Yard, in Westminster, over against the Parliament House, and with a relation of the other traytors which were executed at Worcester.

102. A 19th-century version of The Weekely News, published in what we now regard as January 1605 and reporting the execution of the Gunpowder Plot conspirators.

Saint Paul's Churchyard...' the scaffold having been 'made on purpose for their execution ...'. The *Weekely Newes* reports,

> 'First went up Digby, a man of goodly personage and a manly aspect, but with a vain and superstitious crossing of himself he betook himself to his Latin prayers, mumbling to himself, refusing to have the prayers of any but the Roman Catholicks, went up the ladder, and with the help of the hangman, made an end to his wicked days in this world. After him Winter went up the scaffold, and staid not long for his execution. Then came Graunt, who followed him, showing how so bloody a religion can make such bloody consciences. Then came Bates, and when he was

103. The principal Gunpowder Plot conspirators.

hanged the Executioners prepared to Draw and Quarter them; and when this was done the business of the day was ended.'

The Churchyard was also the scene of the execution of Father Garnet, another possible Gunpowder Plot conspirator – there was some doubt that he had been part of the plot, or if he was, he had been certain that it would not be carried out. On 3 May, 1606 Garnet was placed on a hurdle, and brought here. Garnet who had spent nearly three months in the Tower, said a courteous good-bye to those who had served him. The hurdle was drawn by three horses from the Tower while Garnet lay on it with his hands held together and his eyes closed in prayer, through streets lined with onlookers.

The execution took place at the western end of the churchyard opposite the Bishop's Palace. Attending Garnet, concerned that he should express regret that an attempt had been made on the king and his authority, were the Recorder of London, the Dean of St. Paul's, and the Dean of Winchester. They had been instructed by the King 'to assist Garnet with such advice as suited the condition of a dying man.' The scaffold was built higher than usual so that the assembled crowd could enjoy the spectacle, and hear the condemned man express his regret. There are differing accounts as to how Garnet met his death. Those sympathetic to him portray Garnet as a quiet, resigned martyr bravely meeting his fate. The account in *State Trials*, though biased in the reporting of the execution, has more than a ring of truth about it. Garnet mounted the scaffold looking 'much amazed, fear and guiltiness appearing in his face...The Dean of Paul's and Winchester being present, very gravely and Christianly exhorted him to a true and lively faith to God-ward, a free and plain acknowledgement to the world of his offence, and if any further treason lay in his knowledge, to unburden his conscience, and show a sorrow and detestation of it: but Garnet, impatient of persuasions, and ill-pleased to be exhorted by them, desired them not to trouble him, he came prepared and was resolved.'[1]

Garnet was then led to the corner of the scaffold by the Recorder of London to make his confession and apologies to the surrounding crowd. Garnet was reluctant to make any further statement of repentance and in any case said that his voice was affected and would not be heard. The Recorder responded:

"Mr. Garnet, if you will come with me, I will take care that they shall hear you," and, going before him, led him to the western end of the scaffold. He still hesitated to address the people, but the Recorder urged him to speak his mind freely, promising to repeat his words aloud to the multitude. Garnet then addressed the crowd as follows:

> "My good fellow-citizens, I am come hither, on the morrow of the invention of the Holy Cross, to see an end of all my pains and troubles in this world. I here declare before you all that I consider the late treason and conspiracy against the State to be cruel and detestable; and, for my part, all designs and endeavours against the king were ever misliked by me; and if this attempt had been perfected, as it was designed, I think it would have been altogether damnable; and I pray for all prosperity to the king, the queen, and the royal family."

Here he paused, and the Recorder reminded him to ask pardon of the King for that which he had attempted. "I do so," said Garnet, "as far as I have sinned against him – namely, in that I did not reveal that whereof I had a general knowledge from Mr. Catesby, but not otherwise." Then said the Dean of Winchester, "Mr. Garnet, I pray you deal clearly in the matter: you were certainly privy to the whole business." "God forbid!" said Garnet; "I never understood anything of the design of blowing up the Parliament House."

A key fact at his trial was that he had heard the confession of the proposed plot from one of the conspirators, did not reveal it to the authorities, and was therefore privy to the plan. Garnet claimed that what he heard in confession was private, and not to be repeated. This matter came up on the scaffold:

104. The column in St Paul's Churchyard marks the site of St Paul's Cross, which was removed in 1643. It was in this vicinity that the Gunpowder Plot conspirators met their ends.

"Nay," responded the Dean of Winchester, "it is manifest that all the particulars were known to you, and you have declared under your own hand that Greenaway told you all the circumstances in Essex." "That," said Garnet, "was in secret confession, which I could by no means reveal." Then said the Dean, "You have yourself, Mr. Garnet, almost acknowledged that this was only a pretence, for you have openly confessed that Greenaway told you not in a confession, but by way of a confession, and that he came of purpose to you with the design of making a confession; but you answered that it was not necessary you should know the full extent of his knowledge."[2]

It is likely that Garnet was slowing events in the belief that he would be reprieved in time. There had been rumours in London that the execution would not take place:

> 'Then addressing himself to execution he kneeled to pray. When he stood up, the Recorder finding in his behaviour as it were an expectation of pardon, wished him not to deceive himself, nor beguile his own soul, he was come to die, and he must die. He required him not to equivocate with his last breath; if he knew anything that might be a danger to the King or State, he should now utter it. Garnet replied that he did not now equivocate, and more than he had confessed he did not know.'[3]

Garnet then ascended the ladder and prayed. It was whilst he prayed that the ladder was pulled away. He was fortunate in that a number of those present rushed forward to pull on his legs to ensure he was dead before being quartered.

Location of the Scaffold

The area of St Paul's Churchyard was then more extensive than today. Some accounts of executions place the scaffold at the western end and in Garnet's case we know that he met his death at the western end, opposite the bishop's palace, a building which no longer exists, but was situated within the walls of the churchyard on the north-west side 'upon the spot called London House Yard, now a passage from St Paul's Churchyard to Paternoster Row.' That would place the gallows somewhere in the immediate vicinity of St Paul's Cross.

1 *State Trials*, James I, pp. 356-357

2 Walter Thornbury, *Old and New London*, Vol. 1 (1878), pp. 262-274.

3 John Smith and Charles Mackay, *Streets of London* (1861 edn), p 335

CHAPTER TWELVE

Smithfield

Smithfield is situated within walking distance of the former Newgate Gaol, and was once a primary place of execution.

Stow, writing in 1598, says of Smithfield that '... in a place then called the Elms ... this had been the place of execution for offenders ... Since the which time the building there hath been so increased that now remaineth not one tree growing. Stow describes an area then given over to fairs, celebrations and jousting.

One of the first executions recorded at Smithfield is that of a William FitzOsbert. otherwise known as 'Longbeard'. who was hanged at the Elms in Cow Lane in 1196. And it was at Smithfield that the final act of the Peasants' Revolt of 1381 took place when its leader, Wat Tyler, met the fourteen-year-old king Richard II there for 'negotiations'. Contemporary reports of the event are unreliable and vary, but the general tenor is that Tyler approached the

105. Smithfield c.1576. The church of St Bartholomew the Great is in the centre.

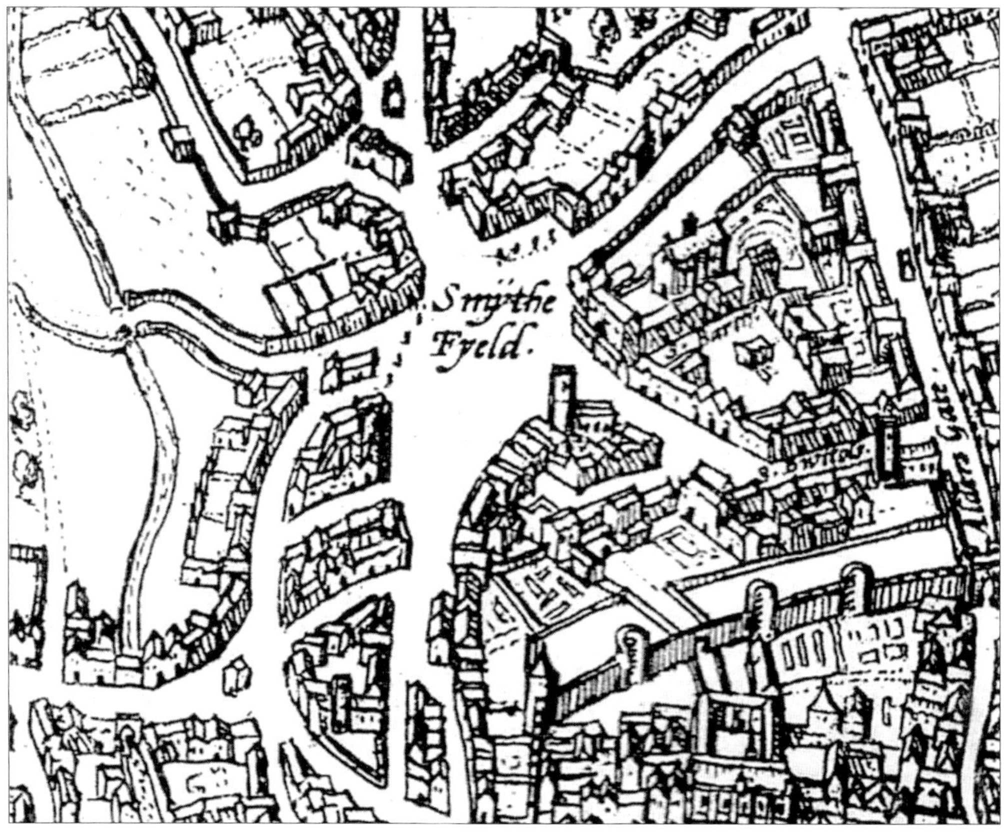

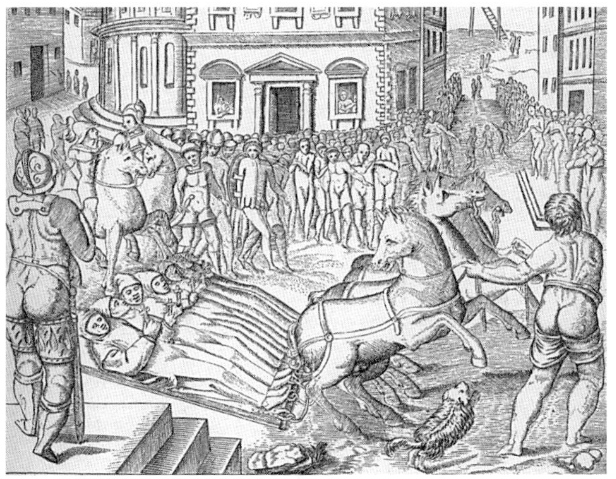

106. Monks at Charterhouse had strongly opposed the remarriage of Henry VIII and his claim to be Supreme Head of the Church in England. The prior was executed at Tyburn in 1535 and ten others in 1537 were imprisoned and tortured in Newgate. Others were burnt at Smithfield.

107. This print of the burning of martyrs at Smithfield has no date, but it might well depict the burning of six people in 1540, three of whom were Protestants and the other three Catholic.

king on horseback in an 'insolent manner', throwing his dagger in the air, and attempted to grab hold of the reins of the king's horse. At this Sir William Walworth, the mayor of London, alarmed that the king would be harmed, ran his sword through Tyler's neck, whilst another attendant of the king leapt at Tyler, stabbing him in the side. Tyler was taken by some of the rebels either into the church of St. Bartholomew the Great or else into St Bartholomew's Hospital, but he was almost immediately dragged out again and beheaded.

A 19th-century history of Smithfield describes it as the place where 'that swollen Ahab, Henry VIII, burnt poor wretches who denied his ecclesiastical supremacy; here Mary burnt Protestants, and here Elizabeth burnt Anabaptists.' This was where 'in 1539 Forest, an Observant friar, was cruelly burnt in Smithfield, for denying the king's supremacy, Latimer preached patience to the friar, [whilst] he hung by the waist and struggled for life.....' [1]

108. During the Marian persecution of Protestants, Anne Askew, John Laceles, John Adams and Nicolas Belenian were burnt at Smithfield, depicted above.

Executions

Many of the burnings for heresy took place during the short reign of Mary I, 1553-1558. A comprehensive description of the lives and deaths of a presumed 278 Protestant deaths during this period may be found in John Foxe's *Book of Martyrs* published in 1563. The book is very anti-Catholic. One execution of particular note was that of John Rogers, vicar of the nearby St Sepulchre, on 4 February 1555. Rogers, a Lutheran, had been held in Newgate prison for heretical preaching; furthermore he had also over the years edited the translation, mainly by Tyndale and Coverdale, of the bible from Latin into English. On the way to Smithfield he asked the Bishop of London, Bonner, his chief persecutor if he might have the single favour 'that I might talk a few words with my wife before my burning.' Bonner refused. He was delivered at Newgate into the hands of the two sheriffs of London. One of them, Woodroofe asked Rogers if he would 'revoke his abominable doctrine' and his 'evil opinion of the sacrament?' 'That which I have preached I will seal with my blood.' Woodroofe, as if in justification of what was to follow responded that Rogers was a heretic and he would not pray for him. Rogers is reported as responding, 'But I will pray for you,' After being tied to the stake, he was offered a pardon on condition that he renounced his heresy. Rogers refused and the pyre was lit. Foxe reports that

> 'when [the flames] had taken hold both upon his legs and shoulders, he, as one feeling no smart, washed his hands in the flame as though it had been in cold water. And, after lifting up his hands unto heaven, not removing the same until such time as the devouring fire had consumed them,

109. In 1555, John Rogers, vicar of St Sepulchre and father of eleven children, was burnt at Smithfield for heretical views.

most mildly this happy martyr yielded up his spirit into the hands of his heavenly Father.

Boiling at Smithfield

There are two executions mentioned in *Stow's Chronicles*, in which the victims were boiled to death at Smithfield. One concerned Richard Rose, a cook at the Bishop of Rochester's palace who had been accused of poisoning 'a diverse number of persons to the number of sixteen or more ... among the which Benet Curwine, gentleman, was one, and he intended to poison the bishop himself, but he ate no pottage that day, whereby he escaped; but of the poor people that ate thereof many died." On 5 April 1532 Rose was boiled at Smithfield for causing the death of sixteen people. The other person to undergo boiling at Smithfield was Margaret Davy, described as a maid, boiled for 'poisoning three households that she dwelled in.'

Of the gallows, Stow says that executions took place between 'the horsepond and Turnmill brook', but there is no indication on early maps where either of these were situated. It is likely, however, that they were located in the central area of Smithfield, probably where the gardens are now.

110. A memorial to martyrs in Smithfield, in the wall of St Bartholomew's Hospital. The inscription reads: 'within a few feet of this spot, John Rogers, John Bradford, John Philpot, and other servants of God, suffered death by fire for the faith of Christ in the years 1555, 1556, 1557.

111. Memorial at Smithfield to the Scots leader, William Wallace. Wallace was probably executed at Tyburn rather than Smithfield.

[1] Walter Thornbury, *Old and New London,* Vol. 2, (1878), pp. 339-344.

CHAPTER THIRTEEN

Wapping

Execution Dock at Wapping was on the Thames about a mile to the west of the Tower of London. Finding Wapping Old and New Stairs needs a methodical approach: that of walking down the high street on the Thames side until one finds the gaps between the buildings. Some care is needed as Wapping Old Stairs is still open to the Thames, and can be wet and slippery. The solitude of the place is rewarding and it is not difficult with the aid of 17th- and 18th-century engravings to picture the crowds, the smells, and the noise of those days. Wapping tube station is in the immediate vicinity as are the two famous pubs, the Prospect of Whitby and the Captain Kidd, vying in their claims to be on the site of the gallows.

Of Wapping, in 1598 Stow tells us in his *Survey of London*:

> 'From this precinct of St. Katherine to Wapping in the Wose (Wash) the usual place of execution for hanging of pirates and sea rovers, at the low water mark, and there to remain till three tides have overflowed them was never a house standing

112. Wapping High Street and the Captain Kidd pub in 2007. Further along on the left are Wapping Old Stairs which lead down to the foreshore.

within these forty years; but since the gallows being after removed farther off, a continual street or filthy strait passage with alleys of small tenements, or cottages built, inhabited by sailors victuallers along by the river of Thames a good mile from the Tower.

Executions at Wapping

Executions at Wapping were just as laden with ritual as those at Newgate and Tyburn. A magazine article of 1844 described the procedure:

'Execution Dock, at Wapping, was devoted to the punishment of such criminals as had been guilty of capital offences on the "high seas." It was not uncommon, and from its frequency, scarcely considered a shocking, occurrence in the streets of London, to meet a wagon, or rather, what is called a "Thames-street cart," moving at a slow pace along the street, and conveying some unhappy culprit to the place of execution. The cart contained also the offender's coffin placed before his eyes, and the chaplain, praying aloud, and exhorting him to repentance. The mournful procession, in which a silver oar, and other symbols of authority, was exhibited, surrounded by a crowd of idlers, arrived at Execution Dock, and in a few minutes the convict was seen struggling between life and death. The tide beneath the criminal was nearly at its lowest ebb, when the executioner cast him off, and the body had to remain until the river touched his feet: sometimes it was allowed to reach his knees. It was then cut down, and placed in the same cart, with a piece of black cloth flung carelessly across it, paraded through the city, and deposited in Hicks' Hall. For the next week the body of the unhappy convict lay for the inspection of the curious and sight-seeing public, cut and mangled, dissected and anatomised – a sickening spectacle to the multitude who crowded to see it, and linger in the gallery to cast down one more look upon the revolting scene ... When every seeker of medical knowledge, from the experienced surgeon to the thoughtless student, had dabbled in the blood of the criminal, the body, mangled and hideous as it was to view, was loaded with chains, and suspended from one of the gibbets which lined the banks of the river in the olden time. "That is my old messmate, Tom Brown," or, "There hangs my fellow-apprentice, Jack Smith," the sailors would say, as they passed down the Thames. Every corpse, disfigured and mutilated though it was, was well known; and as the watermen rowed their boats along the river, they would occasionally pull a little out of their way, to drive off the birds that were greedily devouring the body of some old companion.'[1]

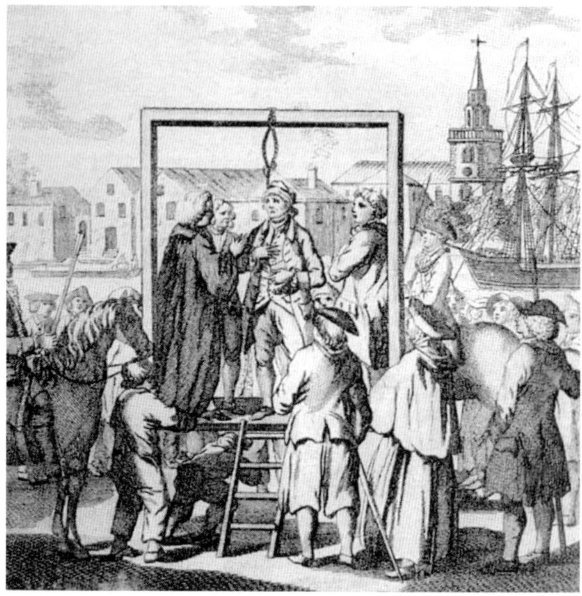

113. *A pirate execution depicted in* The Newgate Calendar.

An entry in Henry Machyn's diary records that on the '6th day of April [1557] was hanged at the low-water marke at Wapping beyond saint Katherines 7 [persons] for robbing on the sea.'

In *Mist's Weekly Journal* of 14 May, 1726:

'Yesterday Captain Jeane was hang'd at Execution-Dock, for the barbarous murther of his cabbin-boy, and was afterwards hang'd in chains on the river-side, over against Cuckold's Point. When the time of his suffering this deserved death drew nigh, he often fell into such violent fits in Newgate, that 'twas thought he would have died there.'

114. *The corpse of Captain Kidd hanging in chains at Wapping in 1701.*

One of the best known executions to take place at Wapping was that of Captain William Kidd (*c*.1645 – 23 May 1701) for murder and five counts of piracy. Kidd at his Old Bailey trial protested his innocence and petitioned the reigning monarchs, William and Mary, but to no avail. Papers that might possibly have saved him had been misfiled, and did not come to light until the 20th century in the Public Record Office. Kidd and a number of colleagues were sentenced to be hanged at Execution Dock on 23 May 1701. Eight of his colleagues received reprieves, but Kidd and one of his crewmen, Darby Mullins, had their sentences confirmed.

They were taken to Wapping in a pair of horse-drawn carts led by the Admiralty marshal carrying the silver oar through a large London crowd. As the *Newgate Calendar* observes, 'a circumstance happened at his execution that will be worthy of recital ...

115. *View from by the Captain Kidd pub today, which compares with Illustration 113. It seems likely that the gallows were by Wapping New Stairs.*

> 'After he had been tied up to the gallows, the rope broke, and he fell to the ground; but being immediately tied up again, the ordinary, who had before exhorted him, desired to speak with him once more; and on this second application, entreated him to make the most careful use of the few farther moments thus providentially allotted him for the final preparation of his soul to meet its important change. These exhortations appeared to have the wished-for effect; and he was left, professing his charity to all the world, and his charity to all the world, and his hopes of salvation through the merits of his redeemer.'[2]

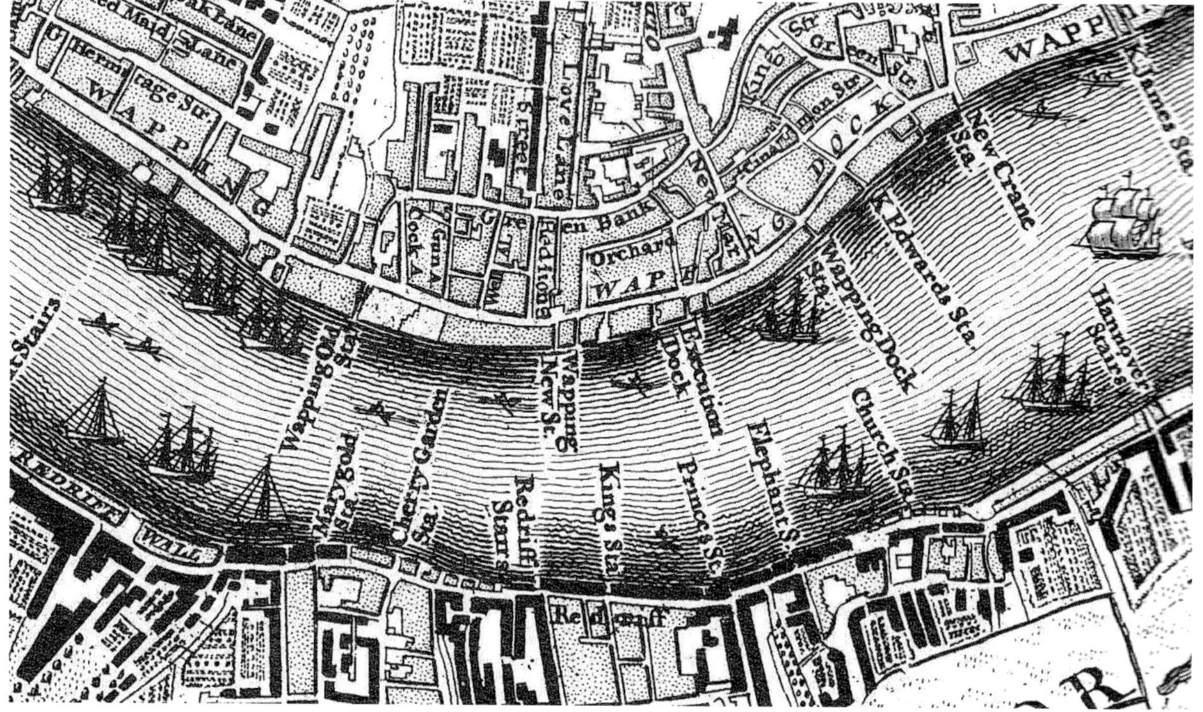

116. Rocque's map of 1746 shows Execution Dock to be a short distance to the east of Wapping New Stairs.

Location of the gallows

The comment by Stow that the gallows had been removed 'farther off' indicates that they had no fixed point, and were set up in the area between the modern day pubs, the Captain Kidd and the Prospect of Whitby in Wapping High Street. *Old and New London* observes that:

> 'Pirates were hung at East Wapping as early as the reign of Henry VI., for in a "Chronicle of London," edited by Sir Harris Nicolas, we read that in this reign two bargemen were hung beyond St. Katherine's, for murdering three Flemings and a child in a Flemish vessel; "and there they hengen till the water had washed them by ebbying and flowyd, so the water bett upon them." And as late as 1735 we read in the *Gentleman's Magazine*, "Williams the pirate was hanged at Execution Dock, and afterwards in chains at Bugsby's Hole, near Blackwall." Howell, in his *Londinopolis*, 1657, says, "From the Liberties of St. Katherine to Wapping, 'tis yet in the memory of man, there never was a house standing but the gallowes, which was further removed in regard of the buildings. But now there is a continued street, towards a mile long, from the Tower all along the river, almost as far as Radcliffe, which proceedeth from the increase of navigation, mariners, and trafique."'[3]

The comparison of the 18th-century engraving in illustration 113 with the modern view in illustration 115, suggests the location of the gallows was close to Wapping New Stairs, near the Captain Kidd public house.

Rocque's 1746 map of London gives Execution Dock as approximately 200 yards east of Wapping New Stairs. It is possible that this was an access point from the New Stairs.

Contemporary accounts speak of the bodies of dead pirates hanging on gibbets which lined the entrance to east London on the river itself. The Rocque map shows two pairs of these gibbets.

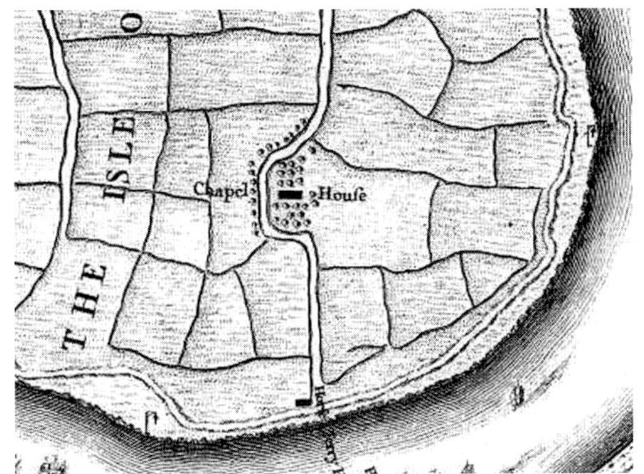

117. Two gibbets on the Isle of Dogs which were used to display hanged pirates. One is bottom left, the other far right.

1 *The Mirror of Literature, Amusement, and Instruction*. New Series. Vol.V pp. 299-300

2 *The Newgate Calendar*. (Folio Society, 1951), pp. 21-22

3 Walter Thornbury, *Old and New London*, Vol. 2 (1878), pp. 128-37.

118. The riverfront today with the Captain Kidd pub to the right. The gallows were probably located at the near end of the picture in the vicinity of Wapping New Stairs.

CHAPTER FOURTEEN

Kennington Common

Kennington is approximately two miles south of Westminster via Westminster Bridge. The former place of execution was directly opposite today's Oval tube station on a site now occupied by St Mark's church. Between 1678 and 1799, 129 executions are recorded there.

The first we know about was that of Sarah Elston who was burned in 1678 for having murdered her husband. The last was that of a fraudster named Badger who was hanged in 1799.

Location of Gallows

The *Survey of London* volume for the area (1956) notes that:

> 'The common land in Kennington lay on the south-eastern border of the Manor, and is now covered by St. Mark's Church and burial ground, the triangle of land between Brixton and Kennington Park Roads, and a large part of Kennington Park. In the 18th and 19th centuries Kennington Common gained an evil reputation. Part of it, including the site of the church and burial ground and the triangle of land between Brixton and Kennington Park Roads, was used as a place of execution and known as Gallows Common. Several Jacobites were executed here after the rising of 1745, and in 1866 when the removal of Temple Bar from Fleet Street was being considered, there was a suggestion that it should be re-erected in the Park to commemorate their execution.[1]

The Common is described in *Tour round London* in 1774 as 'a small spot of ground on the road to Camberwell, and about a mile and a half from London. Upon this spot is erected the gallows for the county of Surrey; but few have suffered here of late years.'[2]

Some Kennington Executions

Kennington Common is best known as the place in which a number of Scottish rebels from the 1745/6 rebellion were executed: an account of the manner in which they were dealt with survives:

119. Rocque's map of 1746 showing the location of Kennington Common and the gallows – opposite today's Oval Underground station.

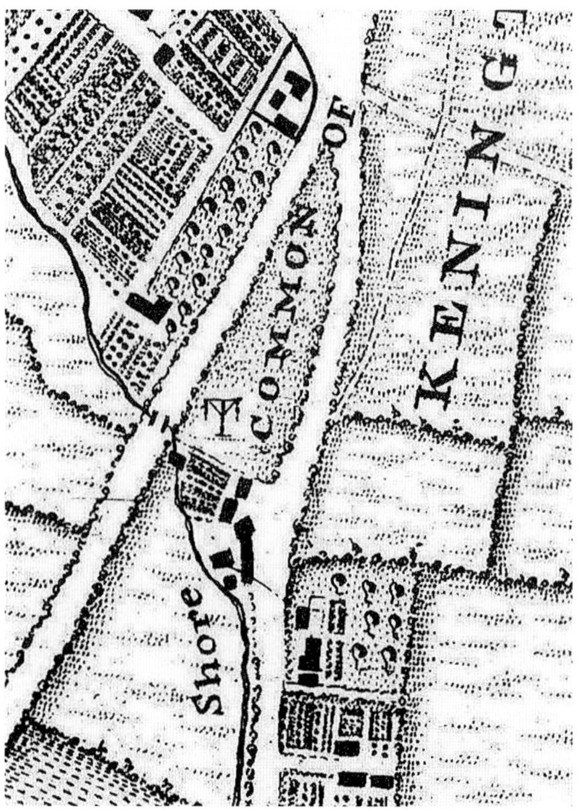

120. St Mark's church, Kennington, on the site of the gallows.

121. The Methodist preacher George Whitfield at the Kennington gibbet c.1748.

'Dawson and eight others were dragged on hurdles from the new gaol in Southwark to Kennington Common, and there hanged. After being suspended for three minutes from the gallows, their bodies were stripped naked and cut down, in order to undergo the operation of beheading and embowelling. Colonel Towneley was the first that was laid upon the block, but the executioner observing the body to retain some signs of life, he struck it violently on the breast, for the humane purpose of rendering it quite insensible for the remaining portion of the punishment. This not having the desired effect, he cut the unfortunate gentleman's throat. The shocking ceremony of taking out the heart and throwing the bowels into the fire was then gone through, after which the head was separated from the body with a cleaver, and both were put into a coffin. The rest of the bodies were thus treated in succession; and on throwing the last heart into the fire, which was that of young Dawson, the executioner cried, "God save King George!" and the spectators responded with a shout. Although the rabble had hooted the unhappy gentlemen on the passage to and from their trials, it was remarked that at the execution their fate excited considerable pity, mingled with admiration of their courage. Two circumstances contributed to increase the public sympathy on this occasion, and caused it to be more generally expressed. The first was the appearance at the place of execution of a youthful brother of one of the culprits, of the name of Deacon, himself a culprit, and under sentence of death for the same crime, but who had been permitted to attend the last scene of his brother's life in a coach along with a guard. The other was the fact of a young and beautiful woman, to whom Dawson had been betrothed, actually attending to witness his execution, as stated above.'[3]

[1] *Survey of London*, Vol. 26: *Lambeth: Southern area* (1956), pp. 31-6.

[2] Quoted in Edward Walford, *Old and New London*, Vol. 6 (1878), pp. 327-41

[3] *Ibid*, p. 340.

CHAPTER FIFTEEN

Hounslow Heath

Despite the dominating presence of Heathrow Airport, there is still a rural atmosphere about Hounslow Heath. It was once the location of numerous highway robberies and of executions. Until 1809, the area was dotted with gibbets, erected as a deterrent.

Edward Walford's *Greater London* of 1883 noted that Hounslow Heath was at one time the chief rival to Finchley Common in the *Lives of the Highwaymen*[1] one of the many eighteenth- and nineteenth-century volumes that delighted in tales of England's 'gentlemen of the roads' whilst pretending to be morality tales. Highway robberies were frequent here from the 17th century and as a consequence provided much material for both the *Newgate Calendar* and the gallows. A historian in 1836 commented that

> "Much less than a century ago the great thoroughfares near London, and above all, the open heaths, as Bagshot and Hounslow, were infested by robbers on horseback, who bore the name of highwaymen ... In the reign of George the First they stuck up handbills at the gates of many known rich men in London, forbidding any one of them, on pain of death, to travel from home without a watch or with less than ten guineas of money ... Mr.Nuthall, the solicitor and friend of Lord Chatham, returning from Bath in his carriage ... was stopped and fired at near Hounslow, and died of the fright....'[1]

122 Gibbets on Hounslow Heath in the 18th century.

A Hanging on Hounslow Heath

It is possible to identify some places and areas mentioned in accounts of executions. One example is from 1864[2] in which the author, Charles Knight, comments that he 'remembered as a child the murder of a Mr. Mellish by a footpad near the "Magpies", and the hanging of these knights of the road on the common, the scene of their misdeeds.' He continues: 'Between the two roads, near a clump of firs, was a gibbet, on which two bodies hung in chains. The chains rattled; the iron plates scarcely held the gibbet together; the rags of the highwaymen displayed their horrible skeletons within.'

The Magpies may well be the The Three Magpies located on the Bath Road, the A4, which backs on to one of Heathrow's main runways.

According to John Rocque's map of Middlesex *c.*1746, the gibbets stood at the juction of the Bath road and the Staines road (now the A30). Gordon Maxwell, author of *Highwayman's Heath,* helps to identify their location by a number of oblique references. He quotes a diary entry of 1819 by

123. The Three Magpies at Hounslow.

124. Hounslow Heath, despite the noise of aircraft, is now a pleasant rural nature reserve.

Henry Crabb Robinson which recorded that he was assured by his coachman that when he, the coachman was a boy 'the road beyond Hounslow was literally lined with gibbets, on which were in irons the carcasses of malefactors blacking in the sun.' Facing the junction of the A30 and A4, there was once 'was an old mansion called Albemarle House, for some time a boys' school and known as Hounslow Academy.' Maxwell refers to a print of 1804 showing the academy, with the boys drilling in a large playground at the rear of the building and the observation made by another writer that '...it was no doubt then considered good for the boys always to have the "humanising spectacle of the gibbets in front of their eyes!"'[3]

As to when the gibbets were removed, Maxwell comments that,

'The Hounslow Heath gibbets were eventually removed as they were an offence to the Royal Family, who passed this way to Windsor. The exact date of their demolition is uncertain, but it was probably about 1809; anyhow, when Hughson wrote his *Circuit of London* in that year they were gone.'[4]

1 Edward Walford, *Greater London* (Alderman Press reprint 1983), p. 65

2 *Ibid*, p. 65

3 G.S. Maxwell, *Highwayman's heath. The story in fact and fiction of Hounslow Heath in Middlesex* (1935), p. 124

4 *Ibid*, p. 124

CHAPTER SIXTEEN

Other Places

Horsemonger Lane Gaol in Southwark served the county of Surrey. It was constructed between 1791 and 1799 and had the dubious distinction of staging its executions on the flat roof of its gatehouse. It was outside this prison that Dickens, along with a crowd of 30,000, attended the execution of the husband and wife, called Manning, who were hanged on 13 November 1849.

In *Criminal Prisons of London* (1862) the authors detail visits to gaols in the capital. They describe the approach to Horsemonger Lane Prison as by

'a narrow lane ... We enter the gateway of the flat-roofed building at the entrance of the prison, on one side of which is the governor's office, and an apartment occupied by the gate-warder, and on the other is a staircase leading up to a gloomy chamber, containing the scaffold on which many a wretched criminal has been consigned to public execution. The prison contained only one cell for the condemned. The visitor to the prison tells us that the cell 'is about the size of four-cells, supported in the centre with two pillars, and has a stone floor. It is furnished with two iron bedsteads and a washstand in one corner and a water-closet in another. An officer is constantly in attendance night and day when a murderer is confined ...'[1]

125. Executions were held on the roof of the Horsemonger Lane Gaol in Southwark. Depicted here is the hanging in 1803 of Colonel Edward Despard and some of his accomplices, found guilty of treason against George III. The bodies were afterwards decapitated.

The gaol, which was demolished in 1878, accounted for the execution of 131 men and 4 women between 1800 and 1877. Its site is now a park, Newington Gardens, near the Inner London Crown Court.

Early records tantalisingly refer to places of execution which rarely appear on maps. Henry Machyn in his diary entry of 12 April 1554 deals with the fate of Thomas Wyatt's head. It was 'set upon the gallows on *Hay-hyll* beside Hyde park; where did hang 3 men in chains upon a stake....' Foxe's *Book of Martyrs* tells us that in the immediate aftermath of the Wyatt rebellion, gallows were set up in Cheapside, and that on the 13th of February 1554, 'were set up a great number of gallowses in divers places of the city; namely, two in Cheapside, one at Leadenhall, one at Billingsgate, one at St. Magnus church [by London Bridge], one in Smithfield, one in Fleet Street, four in Southwark, one at Aldgate, one at Bishopsgate, one at St. James's park corner, one at Cripplegate: and which gibbets and gallowses, to the number of twenty, there remained for terror of others from the thirteenth of February till the fourth of June and then, at the coming in of King Philip [of Spain], were taken down.'[2]

Gallows were sometimes set up near the scene of the crime. An 1856 history of London[3] mentions, amongst many others, gallows at the end of Catherine Street, near the Strand, set up on 14 September 1741 for the execution of James Hall; of an execution at the foot of Bow Street in 1760; another at Chiswell Street, Finsbury in 1767 and another opposite the end of Panton Street in the Haymarket. In 1786 Joseph Rickard, aged 17, convicted of the murder of William Horseman of Kentish Town, was hanged in Kentish Town Road opposite the victim's house.

It was at the Cheapside gallows that a rather unusual incident took place: a cat was hanged. 'The eighth of April [1554], there was a cat hanged upon a gallows at the cross in Cheap, apparelled like a priest ready to say mass, with a shaven crown. Her two fore-feet were tied over her head, with a round paper like wafer-cake put between them whereupon arose great evil-will against the City of London: for the queen [Mary] and the bishops were very angry withal. And therefore the same afternoon there was a proclamation, that whosoever could bring forth the party that did hang up the cat, should have twenty nobles, which reward was afterwards increased to twenty marks; but none could or would earn it.' The same story appears in Henry Machyn's diary of the period.[4]

Old and New London (1878) gives details of other gallows in London.

'... sixty years before the death of Cromwell [1658] the gallows were frequently erected at the extremity of St. Giles's parish, near the end of the present Tottenham Court Road; while for nearly two centuries the Holborn end of Fetter Lane, within a short distance of Red Lion Square, was no less frequently the place of execution. Indeed, in 1643, only a few years before the exhumation and gibbeting of Cromwell, we find Nathaniel Tomkins executed at this spot for his share in Waller's plot to surprise the City.'[5]

In 1856 the *Gentleman's Magazine* reported that 'at an early date, even when St. Giles's was the regular place [of execution]; ... there were gallows and occasional executions at Shepherd's Bush, when Tybourn succeeded St. Giles.'

The *Grub Street Journal* of 7 May, 1730 reported:

> *April* 30. Yesterday Drumond and Shrimpton, lately hanged in chains on Stamford-hill, were removed with their gibbet to a remote part of the Common, near the place where Joseph Still was hanged in the like manner.

From the *Newgate Calendar* of 1663:

> COLONEL JAMES TURNER, a 'Spendthrift London Merchant, against whom three Robberies from other Merchants were proved.'
>
> Upon being convicted, '... the usual sentence of death was passed on him, and he was executed on the 21st of January, 1663, when he was drawn in a cart from Newgate to the end of Lime Street in Leadenhall Street, and there hanged on a gibbet erected for that purpose, being fifty-three years old.

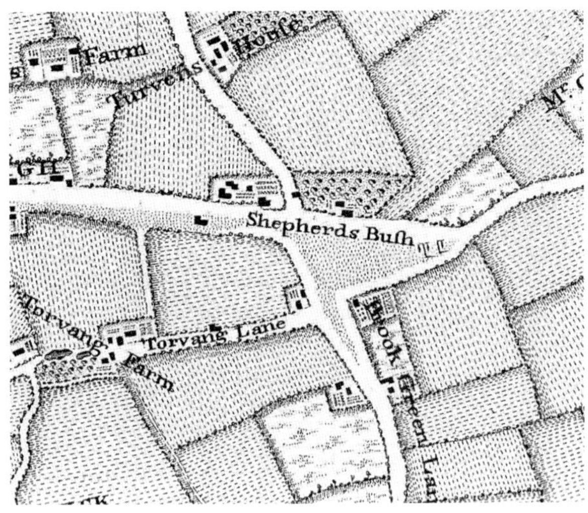

126. Rocque's map of 1746 shows gallows and gibbet at the eastern end of Shepherds Bush Green.Torvang Lane is now the Goldhawk Road and the Holland Park roundabout is about 200 yards to the east of the former place of execution.

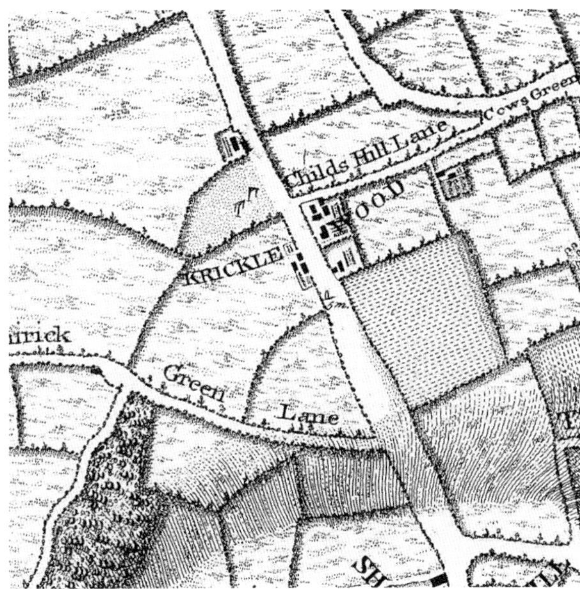

128. Rocque's map of 1746 depicts a double gibbet and a gallows on the corner of Cricklewood Broadway (the Edgware Road) and what is now Chichele Road, NW2. The exact location is probably where Oaklands Road meets the Broadway.

127. The gibbet on Hampstead Heath was strung between these two large elm trees. It was quite near today's Jack Straw's Castle pub, on the left of the road to North End.

The *Newgate Calendar* also refers to the execution of 'JAMES WHITNEY Notorious Highwayman, who believed in dressing well', at 'Porters Block' near Smithfield. (Porter's Block, near Smithfield was in St. John Street.

A 19th century history of London refers to an execution on the corner of Long Lane and Barbican. A memorial stone had been affixed to the cornerstone of a linen-draper's house at the site which read:

> 'On Saturday, Nov. 20, 1790, the two incendiaries were executed, who wilfully set on fire, on the 16th May in the same year, several houses which stood on this ground, and occasioned a loss of upwards of £40,000, for no other purpose but to plunder the sufferes.'

And:

> 'A Person named Flindall, then detected in stealing, wrote a letter to Mr.Alderman Skinner, which led to the disclosure of the whole particulars of that calamity. Flindall being admitted king's evidence, it also appears that this act of villainy had no other object than that of plunder. Edward Love and William Jobbins, being convicted of this crime at the Old Bailey on the 30th October, was executed on the spot where the depredation was committed, on the 20th November, 1790, and confessed their guilt at the place of execution.'[6]

[1] Henry Mayhew and John Binny, *Criminal Prisons of London* (1862), p. 629

[2] John Foxe, *Book of Martyrs*, (1844 edn) p. 1100.

[3] Alexander Andews, *The Eighteenth Century; or, Illustrations of the manners and customs of our grandfathers*, p. 269.

[4] *The Diary of Henry Machyn, Citizen and Merchant-taylor of London, from A.D. 1550 to A.D. 1563*, ed. J. G. Nichols (Camden Society, 1848), p. 59

[5] Edward Walford, *Old and New London*, Vol. 4 (1878), pp. 545-553.

[6] John Smith and Charles Mackay, *Streets of London* (1861), p. 314

Sources and Bibliography

SOURCES

Many of the older sources listed in the bibliography can be accessed on the Internet by way of either Project Gutenberg, or through a Google Books 'full' search. The Google Books often provide scans of the entire original volumes. Additionally many of the early maps of London can be viewed either online or by way of a series of CDs available from Motco who can be found at http://www.motco.com.

Early London maps as superb reproductions created as exact replicas of the originals can be found at www.harrymargary.com.

The website 'The Proceedings of the Old Bailey, London 1674 to 1834' describes itself accurately as a 'fascinating searchable online edition of the largest body of texts detailing the lives of non-elite people ever published, containing accounts of over 100,000 criminal trials held at London's central criminal court.' The project has been led by Professor Tim Hitchcock (University of Hertfordshire) and Professor Robert Shoemaker (University of Sheffield). This site is accessible at http://www.oldbaileyonline.org

BIBLIOGRAPHY

The History of the Press-Yard, or, a brief account of the customs and occurrences that are put in practice ... in that ancient repository of living bodies called ... Newgate, etc, (London).

A. Andrews, *The Eighteenth Century; or, Illustrations of the manners and customs of our grandfathers*,(Chapman & Hall,1856).

Alan Brooke and David Brandon, *Tyburn: London's fatal tree*. (Sutton, Stroud, 2004).

G. Canning and W. R. L. Russell. *An epistle from William Lord Russell: to William Lord Cavendish; written in Newgate, on Friday night, July 20th, 1683*. (London, printed for the author, 1763).

R. B. Challoner, T. G. Law, *et al*. (1742). *Memoirs of Missionary Priests, ... and of other Catholics, ... that have suffered death in England, on religious accounts, from ... 1577 to 1684*. (London, 1741).

R. Chambers, *The book of days : a miscellany of popular antiquities in connection with the calendar including anecdote, biography, and history curiosities of literature and oddities of human life and character*, (W. & R. Chambers, 1869).

The trials of Charles the First, and of some of the regicides : with biographies of Bradshaw, Ireton, Harrison, and others. (Murray, 1839).

J.W. Clayton, *Personal memoirs of Charles the Second : with sketches of his court and times*. (London, Charles J. Skeet, 1859).

W.M.P. Cobbett, T. B. Howell, *et al. Cobbett's Complete Collection of State Trials and Proceedings for High Treason and other Crimes and Misdemeanors from the earliest period to the present time. (vols. 11-21)*. (R. Bagshaw: Longman & Co., 1809).

John Evelyn, *Diary and Correspondence of John Evelyn F R S*. (London, George Bell and Sons, 1881).

John Foxe, *Foxe's Book of Martyrs*, (Protestant Truth Society, London, 1954).

E.A. Freeman and M. Paris, *Chronicles and memorials of Great Britain* (1883).

V.A.C. Gatrell, *The hanging tree: execution and the English people, 1770-1868*. (Oxford University Press, 1994).

D. Gordon, *A general history of the lives, trials, and executions of all the royal and noble personages: that have suffered in Great-Britain and Ireland for high treason, or other crimes, ... Compiled ... from the best histories*. (London, printed for J. Burd, 1760).

D. Hay, *Albion's fatal tree: crime and society in eighteenth-century England*, (Penguin, 1977).

T.S.B. Herbert, R. Lockyer, *et al.* (1959). *The Trial of Charles I. A contemporary account taken from the memoirs of Sir T. Herbert and John Rushworth.* (Folio Society: London, 1959).

Raphael Holinshed, *The firste volume of the chronicles of England, Scotlande, and Irelande, conteyning the description and chronicles of England, from the first inhabiting unto the Conquest. The description and chronicles of Scotland, from the first originall of the Scottes nation, till the yeare 1571. The description and chronicles of Yrelande, from the firste originall, untill the yeare 1547. (The laste volume ... conteyning the chronicles of Englande from William Conquerour untill this present tyme.)* (London: Imprinted for John Harrison,1577).

W.E. Hooper, *History of Newgate and the Old Bailey, etc.* (1935).

C.C.P. Johnson, *A General History of the Lives and Adventures of the Most Famous Highwaymen, Murderers, Street-Robbers, &c. To which is added, a genuine account of the voyages and plunders of the most notorious pyrates. Interspersed with several ... tales and ... songs. Adorned with the heads of the most remarkable villains ... engraven on copper. By Capt. Charles Johnson,* (1734).

C.P. Knight, *Passages of a Working Life during half a century; with a prelude of early reminiscences*, 3 vols. (London, 1864).

Peter Linebaugh, *The London Hanged. Crime and Civil Society in the Eighteenth Century* (Allen Lane, 1991).

Henry Machyn, ed. J. G. Nichols, *The Diary of Henry Machyn, Citizen and Merchant Taylor of London, from A.D. 1550 to A.D. 1563,* (Camden Society, 1848).

B.D. Mandeville, *An Enquiry into the causes of the frequent executions at Tyburn: and a proposal for some regulations concerning felons in prison ... To which is added, a discourse on transportation; and a method to render that punishment more effectual.* (London, J. Roberts, 1725).

A. Marks, *Tyburn Tree: its history and annals,*(London, Brown, Langham & Co., 1908).

G.S. Maxwell, *Highwayman's Heath. The story in fact and fiction of Hounslow Heath in Middlesex, etc.* (Hounslow, Thomasons, 1935).

Henry Mayhew and J. Binny, *The Criminal Prisons of London and scenes of prison life.* (London, 1862).

E. Meteyard, *The hallowed spots of ancient London: historical, biographical and antiquarian sketches, illustrative of places and events made memorable by the struggles of our forefathers for civil and religious freedom.* (1862).

J.G. Nichols ed, *Narratives of the days of the Reformation, chiefly from the manuscripts of John Foxe the Martyrologist; with two contemporary biographies of Archbishop Cranmer,* (1859).

J.G. Nichols ed, *The Chronicle of Queen Jane, and of two years of Queen Mary, and especially of the rebellion of Sir Thomas Wyat. Written by a Resident in the Tower of London.* (London, 1850).

J.G. Nichols and Franciscans, *Chronicle of the Grey Friars of London*, (London, 1852).

Nottingham, H. F. E. *An exact and most impartial accompt of the indictment, arraignment, trial, and judgment (according to law) of nine and twenty regicides the murtherers of His late sacred Majesty of most glorious memory*, (London, 1660).

R.B. Partridge, *'O horrable murder': the trial, execution and burial of King Charles I*, (London, Rubicon, 1998).

C. Pelham, *The Chronicles of crime*, (Miles, 1891).

T. Platter, *Thomas Platter's Travels in England 1599*, (London, Jonathan Cape, 1937).

Roberts, G. , *The Life, Progresses, and Rebellion of James, Duke of Monmouth, to his capture and execution: with a full account of the Bloody Assize, and copious biographical notices*, 2 vols, (London, 1844).

W.S. Scott, *Tales of a grandfather.* (Edinburgh, Robert Cadell, 1849).

D. Shaw, *London in the sixties: (with a few digressions)*. (London, Everett, 1908).

J.T. Smith and C. Mackay. *The streets of London: with anecdotes of their more celebrated residents.* (London, R. Bentley, 1854).

Stanhope, P. H. *History of England from the Peace of Utrecht (to the Peace of Versailles), etc*, 7 vols. (London, 1836)

SOURCES AND BIBLIOGRAPHY

John Stow, *A Survey of London*. (Originally published 1598. Edn. 2005 by Sutton Publishing, Stroud).

Walter Thornbury and Edward Walford, *Old and New London*, 6 vols. (complete by 1878)

P.F. Tytler, *Life of Sir Walter Raleigh.* (Edinburgh, Oliver and Boyd, 1833).

P. F. Tytler, *Life of King Henry the Eighth.* (Edinburgh, Oliver and Boyd, 1837).

Edward Walford, *Greater London*, 2 vols. (Reprinted by Alderman Press, 1984).

Horace Walpole, *The letters of Horace Walpole*, (Bentley and Son, 1891).

INDEX

An asterisk denotes an illustration or caption.